New Fashion from Old

MAUREEN GOLDSWORTHY

B.T. Batsford Ltd *London*

Acknowledgment

I should like to express my indebtedness to Miss Jocelyn Morris, MA, FSA, Director of The Warwickshire Museum Services, for her valuable advice and help in research; to Lever Brothers Ltd. for information on the composition of their products; and to J.H. Plenderleith's standard work of reference, *The Conservation of Antiquities and Works of Art*.

My gratitude is due to Mrs Yvonne Jenner, Mrs Norma Walker and Mr Wilfred Lawson for constructive criticism of text and patterns, and to Vicky Carter and David Jones for the photographs, taken at Warwick Castle by kind permission of Lord Brooke.

Finally I should like to thank most warmly my friends who modelled the clothes: Miss Katherine Harrison-Hall, Miss Rosamund Keer, Mr Andrew Fletcher, the children Fanny Carter and Alexander Wyatt, and my daughter Alice.

© Maureen Goldsworthy 1978
First published 1978

ISBN 0 7134 0913 4

Filmset in Monophoto Garamond by
Servis Filmsetting Ltd, Manchester
Printed in Great Britain by
Butler & Tanner Ltd, Frome, Somerset
for the Publishers B.T. Batsford Ltd
4 Fitzhardinge Street, London W1H 0AH

To M.W.S.G.

New Fashion from Old

Other titles by the author
DRESSMAKING WITH LEATHER
TAKE HALF-A-YARD OF FABRIC
KNOWING YOUR SEWING
KNOWING YOUR DRESSMAKING

Contents

1 Design and Fabric

Have you a good but unwearable dress, nagging at you from the back of the wardrobe? Too short, too tight, or just plain dowdy? If so, this book is written for you. Many people are driven to start dressmaking for exactly this reason – people who like and are accustomed to good clothes, but who have never been particularly good at sewing, or had much time for it.

Your great advantage, as an intelligent adult beginner, is that you already know what you want your clothes to do for you, and what suits your style. This informed taste, and an eye for fashion, are far more important for a successful result than any amount of experience in following paper pattern instructions – experience which you can gain as needed. When you know clearly what you want the finished style to be, then the practical business of achieving it can become surprisingly easy.

Making new fashion from old garments is in any case quite a different skill from starting off with a new length of fabric – and one that is not usually dealt with in dressmaking books. The cut of the garment will be a limiting factor. You can do almost anything with a long, full skirt or a good big tent coat; yet even a dress cut about with bias seams or slot pockets may have possibilities. You must be sure, though, that the strength and substance of the fabric are still good. Worn front edges on a jacket, or worn cuffs or collar, are not difficult to deal with; but watch for any parts that show thin when held up to the light.

There is no lack of incentive, these days. As the prices of everything rise so alarmingly, the ability to make wearable, attractive clothes at virtually no cost must appeal to us all. The sales bargain we longed to buy – but which was a full size too small – may be a perfectly feasible alteration. 'You'd never get material like that now', we say of an old dress or coat; but turned, and restyled, it could be as good as ever it was. 'Just *look* at the price of children's clothes!' – but an outdated adult garment would supply enough fabric, and cost next to nothing. 'It's as good as new, but so *dowdy*' – perhaps a new length, neckline, or type of fastening would lift it into fashion.

1 (Opposite) An evening dress altered from size 12 to size 16 (see pages 31 and 32)

Designing

Good design remains the same whether you are buying, making or altering a garment. It would be pointless just to sew on some new trimming, or change the length of a dress, or chop short a sleeve, without thinking of the design as a whole, and what effect on its balance your alteration will have. The style should always be fully thought through, so that it hangs together as a design.

You need not even end up with the same type of garment. A dress could become a jacket, or you could turn a suit into a dress, trousers into a skirt, or remodel adult clothes into children's. When planning any alteration, then, think of what your wardrobe needs most, rather than restricting your ideas to the smallest possible change.

Figure 1.1

STRIPES AND SHAPES

Horizontal stripes are usually held to be widening, and vertical stripes slimming. This is not always so. It all depends on their proportions. Necklines, seams and hemlines catch the eye in the same way as stripes, so their placing is just as important.

In figure 1.1, the first dress (top left) has contrasting hip and sleeve bands at the same level, which give a strongly horizontal effect. The collar, too, emphasizes this line. It could be becoming on a tall figure with narrow hips; disastrous on a petite, plump one. The second dress (bottom left) has horizontal stripes which are so narrow and close-set that their sheer number seems to elongate the figure; such stripes could well be slimming.

The third dress (top right) has no colour contrast, but the square neck, the belt, and the hip-level seam all tend to draw the eye across the dress. The sleeve style adds width to the neckline. The pleated panel is here so short, in proportion, that it has the effect of a width-ways stripe. A very widening style all the way.

But one might sometimes wish to emphasize width at one point of the figure. In the fourth dress (lower right), the shoulder-line yoke could be excellent for narrow, sloping shoulders, while the two vertical seams, with no break, tend to slim the waist and hips. Each of the four dresses seems to be of a different size: this is an illusion. All the figures are identical.

NECKLINES

Necklines, also, must be thought out with care. Nothing – except the wrong length – will date a dress more firmly than the style and proportions of its collar. Equally, nothing can revive it more quickly than a new one. As well as being cut in a currently fashionable shape, the neckline should flatter. A close or high collar will suit a long, slim neck; a deep V will lengthen a short or plump one, and make the figure seem taller. If you have good shoulders, show them – with a low, wide neckline.

SPARE FABRIC

Any spare pieces of a garment's original fabric may be invaluable in alterations. A strip might be wanted for a new waistband, perhaps – or even a scrap for new bound buttonholes. Never throw away any material while you still have the garment. But there is one point to watch. Any large added parts may look new against the rest. You might need to wash the spare fabric several times, to make a true match.

CONTRASTING FABRIC

In any alteration, except for those merely affecting the size, some contrasting material may be needed. This gives great scope for fashionable detail. Do not play down the contrast, but emphasize it as an important part of the design. The shape of a yoke, for instance, might be echoed by pocket flaps.

The use of a particular colour can bring a dress right up to date, especially the exact white, ivory, fawn or cream that may be the current basic shade. In a 'cream year', you might only have to replace a white collar to give a dress new impact. Whatever may be in vogue – pastels, strong or rich colours, prints or stripes or checks of this season's proportions – can give this season's mark. Quite a small piece of fabric may provide the colour accent to lift a garment into fashion.

Any material may be used. Different textures such as suède, grain leather or jersey may be immensely effective. One's aim, as always, should be to integrate the new material into the design, so that it does not give the impression of being applied as an afterthought. The contrast should be of much the same weight as the original fabric, but the two materials can be quite diverse. In fact, some of the most successful marriages are between:

  tweed and suède
  knit and woven fabrics
  smooth fabrics and grainy ones, such as gaberdine, bouclé or leather
  plain fabrics and boldly patterned ones
  any fabric and the same in a paler or darker shade.

Wide or narrow braid, ribbon or knit trims are also useful as fashion pointers.

Bear in mind future washing or dry-cleaning, though, in your mixture of materials. Leather and suède both clean well; but even washable glove leather or chamois need special handling, and are not satisfactory teamed with a fabric that will often be washed.

Reviving without remaking
When a garment just has a tired air, look first to the fabric rather than the style. Much can be done, without any actual restyling, to restore the shape of the garment or the texture of the fabric.

RESHAPING WITH STEAM

Woollen fibre is elastic, and can stretch out of shape. But luckily it also shrinks; when making a suit, a tailor shapes the shoulder and sleeve-head by steam-pressing and shrinking away the fullness into a smooth rounded line. Steam-pressing is also useful for restoring their original shape to seated skirts, or to sleeves that have gone baggy at the elbows.

For a seated skirt, press on the wrong side with a steam-iron, or through a damp cloth. (Damp means just moist, not sodden.) Work in a circle, from the hem upwards and from the side seams inwards, always moving the iron in towards the centre-back. The bulge will gradually move to the middle, and shrink out (figure 1.2).

If you are setting back the shape into a jacket, press in the curve of the shoulder or bust by working over a small, firm cushion. Tailors use a kapok-stuffed pad; you could make one very simply (on the oven-glove principle) from three pieces of old sheet, each 15 by 20 cm, with selvedges at the opening end (figure 1.3).

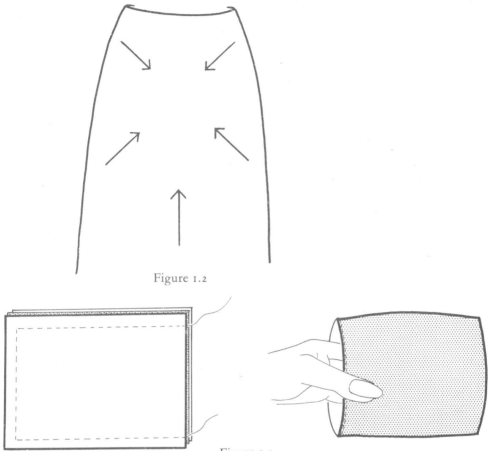

Figure 1.2

Figure 1.3

To sharpen up pleats in a woollen skirt, press each one separately on the inside edge first; then turn the skirt over to the right side, and the outer edges of the pleats will fall easily into place. Press with steam, or over a damp cloth; if you need to, hold the point of each pleat to the ironing board with one pin. Leave the pleats to cool off, before moving to the next section of skirt. They will hold their shape better if given time to set. Another trick is to 'beat in' pleats – hard – with the back of a brush, while they are still hot: one of the few dress-making processes on which one can release pent-up emotion.

Man-made fibres do not stretch or shrink, so on woven fabrics steam-pressing should not be used. But knitted fabrics, particularly double-jersey skirts, can be helped back into shape by pressing on the wrong side with a dry iron. For acrylics (Courtelle, Acrilan, Orlon) use the lowest iron setting, No. 1. As polyesters (Crimplene, Terylene, Dacron) will stand more heat, use No. 2 setting, as for wool. Heat can put a shine on polyester, though, so be sure to press on the wrong side only. Steam or damp pressing cloth should never be used on these man-made fibres.

FABRIC CONDITIONING

A conditioning rinse, such as Comfort or Lenor, gives new life to garments in several ways. It restores softness and body, and does much to prevent felting in woollens. By laying a protective film over each fibre, it improves the handle of all fabrics. It works, in fact, on the same principle as a conditioning rinse at the hairdresser's.

It also eliminates static electricity, and so stops highly-charged man-made fibres from clinging and riding up. Anti-static treatments during manufacture have reduced this problem in most new materials made from nylon and polyester, but you may still meet it in acrylics (such as Orlon), or in garments bought some time ago. It is static which causes discolouration, particularly of white nylon. This, if washed with coloured clothes, may attract from them minute particles which become chemically bonded into the fibre, giving an all-over dullness. White nylon should therefore be washed separately. It should not be allowed to get too grubby before washing, as dirt also may become fixed into the fabric; it is better to wash nylon after each wearing. Here again, a conditioning rinse will help.

Machine-washable wool has been treated during manufacture with a finish which permanently coats the scaly surface of the fibres. This makes them smoother, so that they do not so easily 'ratchet' together and shrink or felt with rubbing. Even so, too much rubbing can damage the finish. Treat washable wool gently, and give it only a short spin-dry.

DRY-CLEANING AND DYEING

Doing-it-yourself For removing spots and stains at home, the old rules still apply.

1 Tackle any mark at once. Old stains are more difficult to shift.
2 Try cold water first, even on a fabric that is not fully washable – working over the stain with your fingers, under a running tap. Tea and coffee respond to this, and some inks. It is the best way to remove protein-based stains, such as blood, which warm water would 'cook' into the fabric. On washable fabrics (except silk), a biological detergent can be used.
3 Use warm water and detergent, if the fabric is washable, to remove most grease stains.
4 Spirit cleaners (such as Dabitoff, Thawpit), or white spirit, will lift oil-based marks, and are safe on any fabric. The difficulty is to avoid leaving a conspicuously clean circle on the garment. First, work with very light strokes, from a distance inwards to the spot. Then go over the mark itself. Have ready a kettle of fast-boiling water; immediately the stain is out, treat the whole area with steam, again working in towards the centre. This is usually effective in 'feathering out' the ring.
5 Be careful with aerosol spot removers. They make no ring, but may leave a pale deposit on dark clothes.
6 Methylated or white spirit will usually remove fresh grass stains.

7 Trichlorethylene is a powerful industrial de-greaser, sometimes used for spotting fabrics. Treat it with great respect. Wear old leather gloves. Do not inhale the vapour; when drawn in through a cigarette, it produces a poisonous gas. This chemical must not be used on man-made fibres.

Professional dry-cleaning Modern dry-cleaning in perchloroethylene ('Perk') is safe for all fabrics that are used for clothing, including the man-made fibres; the only exception is plasticized Vinyl, which in any case one would simply sponge over.

The cleaning of leather and suède garments is for specialists; they need a different cleaning solution, and afterwards are given a number of treatments such as re-oiling and re-tinting. These are not possible for ordinary dry-cleaners; so entrust your leather coat to a specialist firm, or have it cleaned through the agency of the shop from which you bought it. Very dirty garments may need to be put through the cleaning process several times. Even leather may be affected by this; do not let it get too dirty before cleaning. The result will be well worth the expense – a garment almost indistinguishable from new.

Clothes with narrow trims of grain leather or suède can be satisfactorily cleaned by ordinary cleaners.

Dyeing This, too, is a highly specialized process nowadays, undertaken by a few firms only. Natural fibres, such as wool and cotton – even rayon – are porous and readily take dye. Many man-made fibres, in their finished state, will not take dye at all – or only in a parody of the colour wanted.

These fibres are very diverse, ranging from polyester – used not only for clothing, but also as anti-freeze in car radiators – to the fluorocarbons such as Teflon – used for coating both saucepans and re-entry rockets from the moon. But their common feature is that all the fibre surfaces are smooth, hard and impermeable, designed to resist dirt or any foreign substances.

Some are dyed at the solution stage, before the chemical mix has even been solidified into a filament as the first step towards becoming a thread. The dye in this case is totally fast, built into the fibre itself. Or mixtures of two different fibres may be dyed after weaving; the object, where they take dye differently, being to produce a two-colour fabric from only one dyeing operation. Even natural fibres such as cotton or wool, when treated with easy-care or machine-washable resin finishes, may not accept dye evenly. So there are many complications in home-dyeing. One might inadvertently get an almost 'denim' effect from a mixed-fibre material. This is not a do-it-yourself activity, except for such fabrics as cotton lawn, calico or cheesecloth.

Specialist dyers, of course, continue to accept garments made from natural and from some man-made fibres. Wool, cotton, rayon and linen all dye well. Particular weaves, too, such as velvet made from cotton or rayon, come up beautifully.

2 Time-Saving Techniques

The right way in dressmaking – or in any other work – should be the one that achieves precisely the result you want, with the least trouble and in the shortest time. Indeed, that is why it is right. So whenever a seemingly roundabout method is suggested here, perhaps involving extra preparation, the reason is that it will save you time in the end.

A great deal can also be learnt from studying the original construction of a garment. Particularly with knit fabrics and man-made fibres, good manufacturing practice can often reveal new and simple methods – not always to be found in books. These may have been developed because of 'de-skilling' – an ugly word for re-thinking industrial processes; but they may be equally useful to amateur dressmakers.

Preparing to Fit

UNPICKING

This unavoidable first step can be unbearably tedious. Here is the quickest way to unpick safely. Unravel the first five or six stitches. Then, using eyebrow tweezers, tug sharply at one thread, and cut it off close to the fabric. Turn the seam over, and repeat with the loose end on the other side. Even with very small stitching, you should be able to move along 2 to 3 cm at each pull – without any danger of cutting the fabric.

A stitch-ripper can be a help, with the knob-end inserted under the seam. But if used without the utmost caution, it can cut the fabric.

TACKING AND BASTING

You should always try on any garment you are altering, before the final stitching. It is far easier to change a line of tacking than to unpick machining. Tacking (or basting) is a row of stitches used to hold together two layers of fabric, while you try on, and while you machine. Tacking holds best if you space the stitches in pairs (figure 2.1). Be sure to begin securely with a knot and back-stitch – and end with two back-stitches. Tacking that falls apart when you fit is a waste of your time.

Another kind of basting, useful for slippery fabrics or for the exact matching of checks, is worked with stitches at right angles to the seam-line (figure 2.2). This will keep one layer of fabric from creeping up on the other during machining; it is also invaluable for setting in a zip.

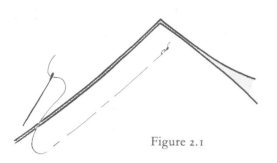

Figure 2.1

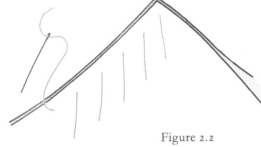

Figure 2.2

PIN-BASTING

As the pinning here is on the right side, it allows an alteration to be made while you are trying on the garment. This is useful for setting the line of a dart or the fit of a sleeve; you can move the pins one by one until you are satisfied. Of course, it is far easier with a friend to do the pinning (figure 2.3).

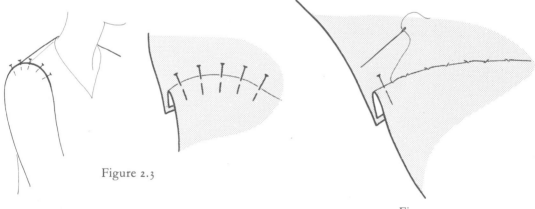

Figure 2.3

Figure 2.4

SLIP-BASTING

After pinning, take off the garment and slip-baste it – still on the right side – exactly along the pinned line. Take stitches alternately on each side of the line, through the single thickness, or through just the very edge of a fold. A friend could do this while you still have the garment on (figure 2.4). When you turn it wrong-side-out, this slip-basting will show as a row of small tacking stitches, ready-placed for machining. A saver of time, and a guarantee of accuracy.

MACHINE BASTING

Machining with the longest stitch you can set. If you are able to machine reliably straight first time, it can be a quick way of basting before trying on. It is easily taken out, just by pulling one thread-end.

Marking with Tailor's Tacks

To match the position of darts, pockets, etc., you will need to mark the left and right sides of a garment simultaneously. There are several ways – with a tailor's chalk block under the double fabric, and a chalk pencil over it; or with a tracing wheel and dressmaker's carbon paper. But tailor's chalk can rub off too soon, and carbon paper may not transfer well on rough-surfaced fabrics. The best way, perhaps, is with tailor's tacks. They have the advantage of staying safely in place.

1 Fold the garment down its centre, so that it can be marked accurately through both layers.

2 With a double thread, take a tiny stitch at the point to be marked. Take another right over it, and draw up the thread to leave a loop just big enough to put your finger through.

3 Move on to the next point, again leaving a loop of thread, and repeat the pair of stitches.

4 To separate the two thicknesses of fabric, first cut the threads between each mark (figure 2.5).

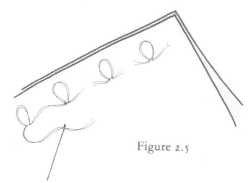

Figure 2.5

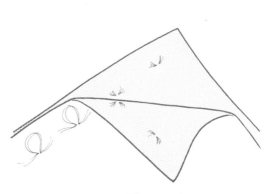

Figure 2.6

5 Then gently ease the two layers apart, and snip the remaining stitches between the layers, leaving a tuft of thread on each (figure 2.6).

Machining

KEEPING STRAIGHT

Keep your stitching parallel to the edge of the fabric by using the distance-marks on the machine needle-plate. Put a tape-measure under the machine-needle, and measure to the right; if you are working to a seam-allowance of 1.5 cm, note the guide-line on the plate that corresponds to that distance (figure 2.7). If your machine has no lines, stick on a piece of Sellotape to guide you. Keep the edge of the fabric level with this line as you stitch – do not watch the needle.

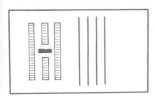

Figure 2.7

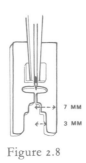

7 MM

3 MM

Figure 2.8

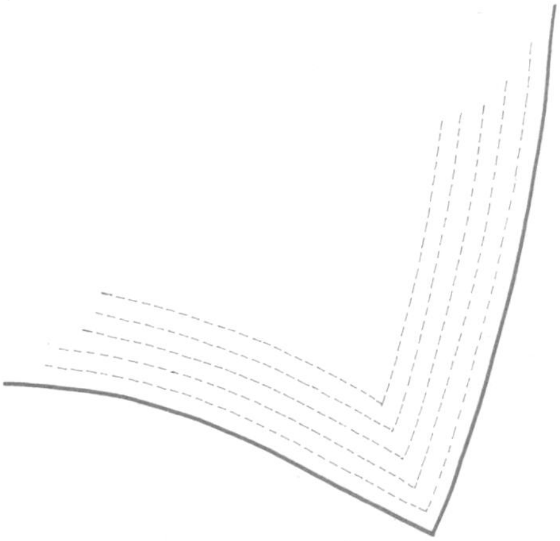

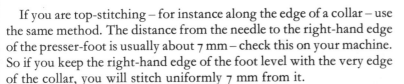

Figure 2.9

If you are top-stitching – for instance along the edge of a collar – use the same method. The distance from the needle to the right-hand edge of the presser-foot is usually about 7 mm – check this on your machine. So if you keep the right-hand edge of the foot level with the very edge of the collar, you will stitch uniformly 7 mm from it.

Other cut-out shapings of the foot will give other, narrower measurements. From the needle to the inner edge of the toe will be about 3 mm (figure 2.8). Successive, close rows of machining can be worked with this placing (figure 2.9). Nothing gives a more professional look than multiple rows of stitching, worked with absolute accuracy – and it is not difficult. Turn corners sharply by leaving the needle down in the fabric, lifting the foot, and pivoting the work round on the needle.

MACHINING OVER PINS

With care, this is another time-saver. If is safe if – and only if – the pins are placed at right angles to the line of machining; if you go slowly; and if the fabric is thick enough to cushion the machine foot as it passes over the pins.

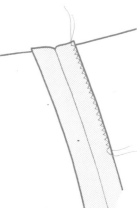

Figure 2.10

MACHINE-NEATENING OF EDGES

To prevent fabric edges from fraying, use the plain zigzag stitch on a swing-needle machine. Let the left-hand stitch bite into the fabric about 3 mm in from the edge, while the right-hand stitch goes just over the edge (figure 2.10).

On thin fabrics, fold under 5 mm along the edge of the seam turning and machine along the fold with a straight stitch (figure 2.11).

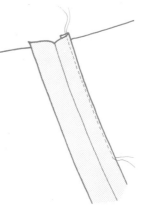

HEMMING BY MACHINE

If your machine has a hemming stitch, do learn to use it. This needs a sensitive touch; but once you have mastered it, it will save much time and give an excellent finish.

Figure 2.11

1 Neaten the raw edge first, with zigzag stitching.
2 Turn up the hem in a single fold, and tack it (figure 2.12a).
3 Fold the hem back over to the right side of the skirt. The hemming is worked along the edge of the turning – five straight stitches, followed by one swinging over to catch in the fold (figure 2.12b and c).

Figure 2.12

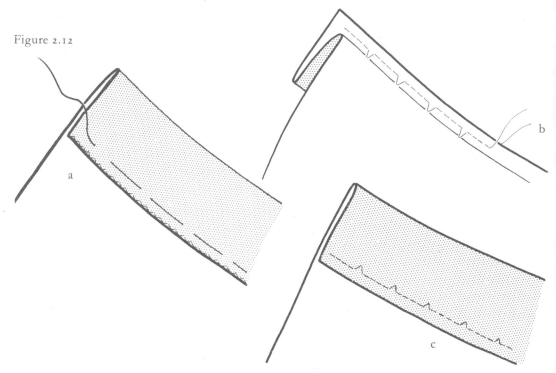

If the stitch is set too narrow, it will miss the fold altogether; if it is too wide, it will leave a long thread showing on the right side. Practise until you can judge exactly – the stitch should be small enough to be invisible on the right side.

MACHINE BINDING AND NARROW-HEMMING
Each of these finishes needs a special foot, with a shaped slot into which the fabric is fed. Once this is in place, the foot will make a perfectly even finish along a straight edge. These feet are not so reliable, though, on sharp curves – and they cannot turn corners. But they are invaluable for long, straight edges such as along frills and flounces. Practise on a scrap of fabric first.

Four Indispensable Hand Stitches SLIP-HEMMING
This is the stitch for invisible hemming. It is used on thin fabrics, where the upper edge of the hem is turned in. Take only a thread or two of the skirt fabric in the needle, but a longer stitch through the fold of the hem. In this way, there will be no long, uncovered stitches

to catch one's heel and pull out. Hem loosely; no line will then show on the right side. One stitch to the centimetre is close enough (figure 2.13).

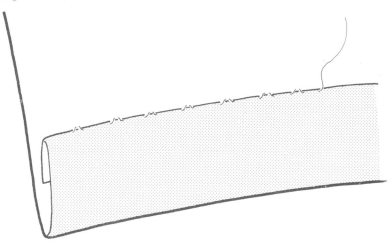

Figure 2.13

CATCH-STITCHING

On thicker fabrics (including all woollens, and acrylic and polyester jerseys) the upper edge of the hem should not be turned in. Strengthen it first with a line of straight or zigzag machining, 3 mm from the edge. Then turn up and tack the hem. Fold it back over against the right side of the skirt, and sew in herringbone fashion between the hem and the wrong side of the skirt. Stitch very loosely – this gives a stretchable finish, and prevents any ridge from appearing on the right side (figure 2.14).

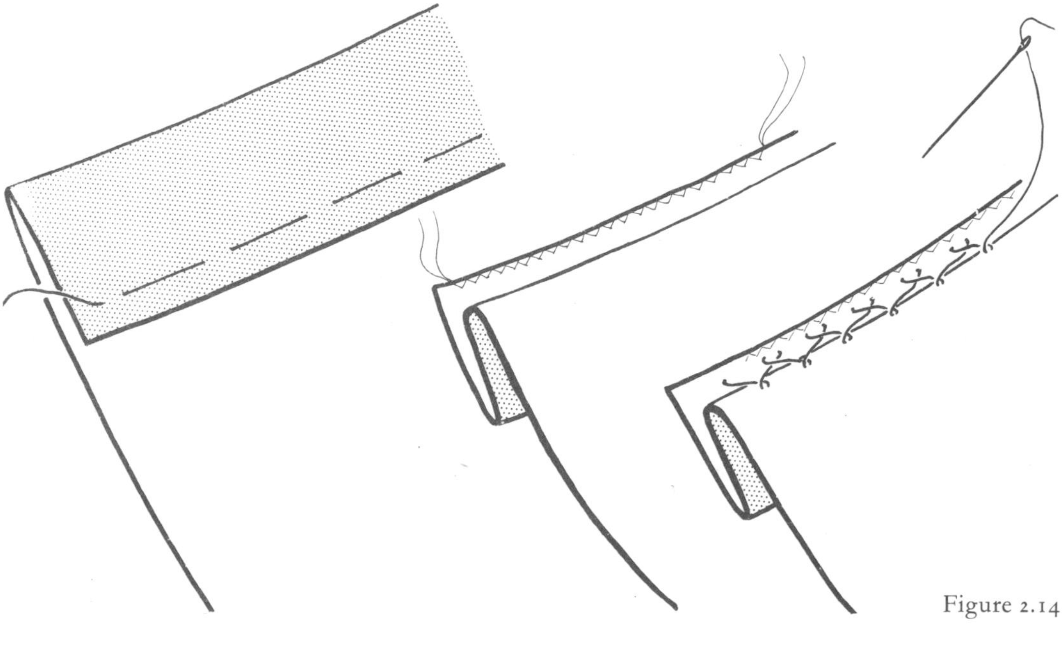

Figure 2.14

FELLING

Felling is especially useful for stitching the lining into a coat or a jacket, or where any folded edge is to be sewn to a single thickness of material. Take a long stitch through the single thickness of the facing, and bring the needle up through the fold of the lining. If you begin each stitch opposite to the last one, it will be almost invisible (figure 2.15).

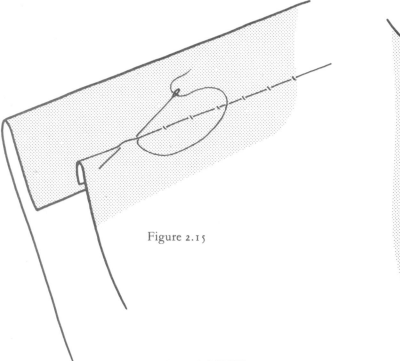

Figure 2.15

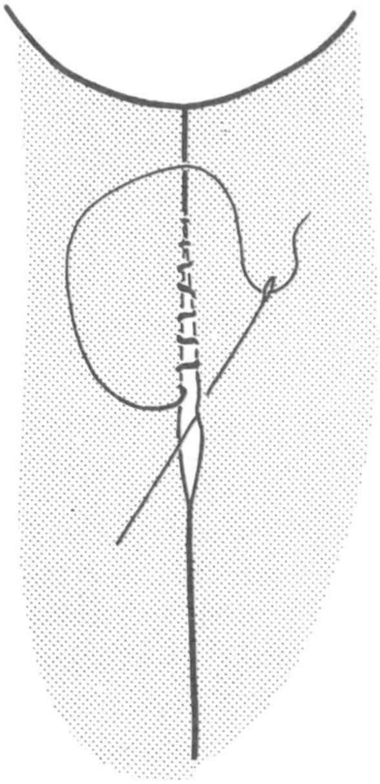

Figure 2.16

DRAWING STITCH

This is a tailoring stitch, used to sew together two folded edges, and worked from the right side of the garment. Use the drawing stitch where you cannot easily reach the wrong side; for instance, to mend a split seam below the armhole of a coat. Begin with a knot or two back-stitches, out of sight on one turning. Take stitches through the edge of each fold alternately, starting each stitch opposite to the last one. Pull up firmly. Finish with three stitches in the same place, and lead away the thread-end inside the fold (figure 2.16).

3 Size Alterations

A hemline of the wrong length may by itself render a dress or skirt **Lengthening**
virtually unwearable; yet there must be few which could not be
lengthened by one or other of these methods.

LETTING DOWN A HEM
The simplest way of all. The depth of the hem, less 1 cm, is the limit
of the extra length available; but even 4–5 cm is a lot in dressmaking.

1 Unpick the hem and press out the crease. Steam-iron, wash or dry-
  clean if necessary, with the hem down, to remove any mark along
  the old hemline.
2 As there will not be so much weight in the new, narrower hem, give
  it a little more substance by finishing it with wide bias binding.
3 Put the binding and fabric right sides together, with their edges
  matching. Machine along the lower crease of the binding (figure
  3.1). Make joins in the binding as shown, with the end of the
  binding folded over diagonally along its straight thread.

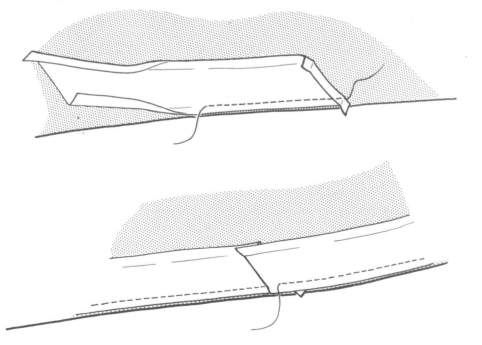

Figure 3.1

4 Press the binding downwards, along the stitching.
5 Now press up the new hem, not less than 1 cm deep to the binding.
6 Slip-hem the upper (folded) edge of the binding to the skirt (figure 3.2).

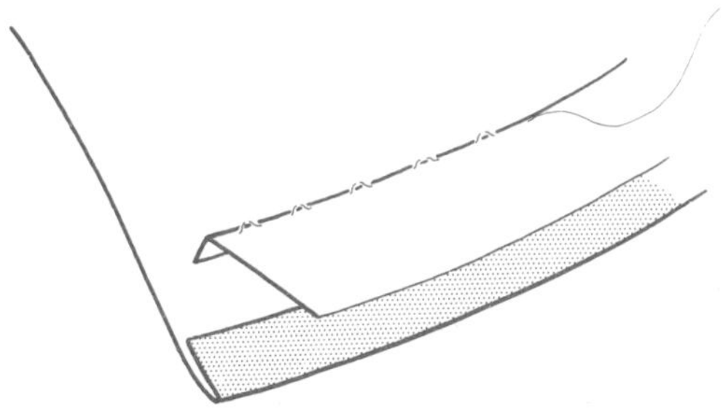

Figure 3.2

As bias binding will stretch and shape into a curve, it can be used on the hems of either straight or flared skirts.

FALSE HEMS

A false hem can be used to obtain the utmost extra length. It also has the advantage of adding weight and substance at the hemline, so improving the hang of the skirt.

1 Unpick the old hem and press out the crease.
2 For the false hem, choose a fabric either matching or nearly matching, in both colour and weight.
3 The false hem for a straight skirt is made from strips cut across the fabric, at right angles to the selvedge. Cut the strips 7–8 cm wide, to allow a turning along the lower edge – and on thin fabrics along the upper edge as well. Their length should allow any joins to coincide with the skirt seams.
4 For a flared skirt, the false hem will need to be shaped to a curve. To make the pattern, lay the skirt out, section by section, over newspaper; pencil along its let-down edge, and mark in the length of each section of skirt from seam to seam. Add 1.5 cm seam allowance at each end. Cut the curved strips of newspaper as deep as you need the hem to be, allowing for turnings. It is worth while cutting out all the false hem sections in newspaper first, to give an easier and more economical layout on the fabric. The straight grain of the fabric should lie vertically at the centre of each strip. This is most important to the smooth setting of the hem (figure 3.3).
5 Seam the hem sections together, and press open the seams.
6 Place the false hem right sides together with the garment, edges matching; and stitch the seam 1 cm or less from the edges. Press open the turnings of this seam, all round the skirt.
7 Now press up the hem into position, making sure that the seamline falls a hairsbreadth towards the inside of the garment. Do not allow the iron to go over the upper edge of the hem, or it may leave a mark on the right side.

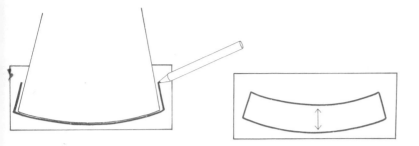

Figure 3.3

8 On thin fabrics, such as voiles or ginghams, the free edge of the hem may be turned in and slip-hemmed, as shown on page 19. On any thicker fabrics (including all woollens and worsteds, and acrylic and polyester knits), the upper edge of the hem should not be turned in. Instead, use catch-stitching. (See page 19.)

SKIRT INSERTIONS
If a false hem is impracticable, or if the worn line along the old hem would show badly, then a possible solution on a straight-cut, pleated or gathered skirt would be to insert a band of contrasting fabric (figure 3.4). (If there is any flare at all in the lower part of the skirt, this is not possible.)
1 Decide the extra length needed. Cut strips of the contrasting fabric this depth, plus 6 cm for the seam turnings on the upper and lower edges. Each strip should be the width of the skirt panel, plus 3 cm.
2 Decide how far above the hem the insertion should be placed. (It is best to leave the old hem unaltered.) As a wide horizontal band will be an important feature of the garment, try out the proportions by pinning a paper pattern of the band across the skirt before actually cutting. The placing may look well if the band and the section of skirt below it are of about equal width.
3 Cut across the skirt, remembering that a seam turning of 1.5 cm will be needed in the lower section (figure 3.5).
4 Unpick the skirt seams for 3 or 4 cm above and below the line you have cut.

Figure 3.4

Figure 3.5

Figure 3.6

Figure 3.7

Figure 3.8

5 Stitch an insertion strip first to each upper panel of the skirt, with 1.5 cm turnings, and then to each lower section (figure 3.6).
6 Lastly, stitch the side and back seams from just above to just below the insertion. This gives firm vertical seaming, and helps the skirt to hang better (figure 3.7).

WAISTLINE INSERTIONS

A dress of any cut – straight, pleated or flared – can be lengthened by letting in a band at waist level. This may be most effective if its finished width is about 10 cm, half above and half below the true waistline. It could be cut straight, or shaped in slightly at the side seams (figure 3.8).
1 To drop the skirt, unpick any waist seam, and the top few centimetres of the skirt seams. Release the lower end of any zip.
2 Trim off as much as you wish from the waist edge of the bodice, remembering to leave a 1.5 cm seam allowance.
3 Seam the insertion sections to bodice and skirt panels.
4 Stitch the side and back seams, taking in slightly smaller turnings at the top of the skirt to allow for its new, lower level over the hips.
5 Reset the lower end of the zip.
6 A narrow belt and belt-carriers (see page 52) could add emphasis to this style.

LENGTHENING A FLARED SKIRT WITH A HEM-BAND

Although the shaping of a flared skirt precludes any insertion, length could still be added by a band extending below the hem edge. Let down the hem, and use the edge as a pattern, over newspaper, to draw in the shape of this band. Because of the curve, the pattern should be cut to overlap the skirt edge by 3 cm (figure 3.9), to give the seam allowances.

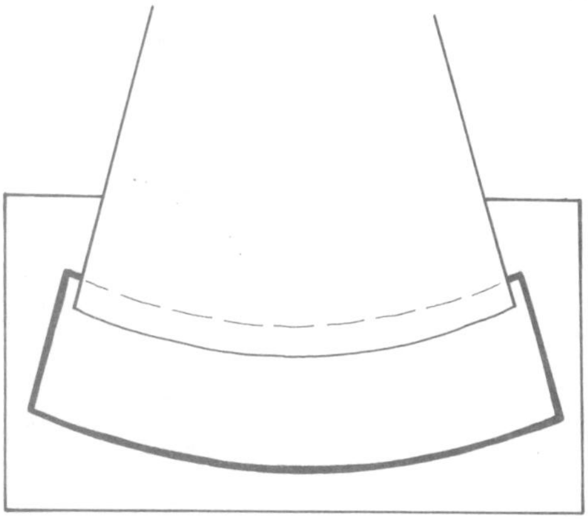

Figure 3.9

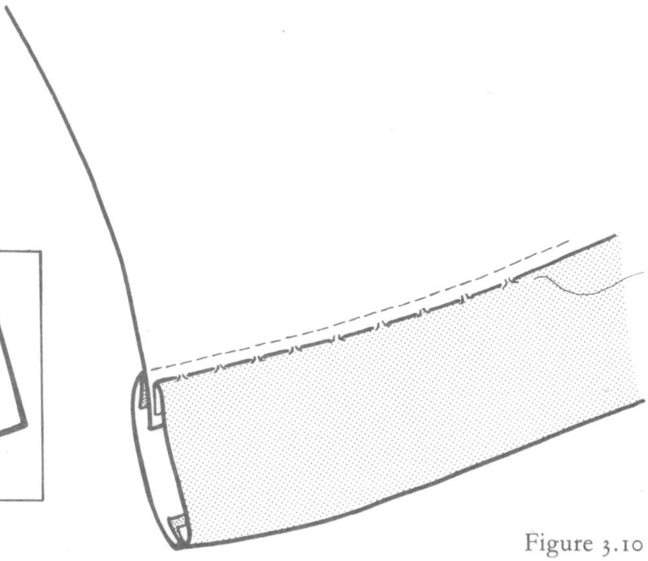

Figure 3.10

As well as the band, cut a facing to the same pattern. When this is stitched in place (like the false hem on pages 22–3), it can be finished by slip-hemming to the upper seamline of the band (figure 3.10). This will add weight at the hemline and improve the hang of the skirt.

The only drawback to this method of lengthening is that it takes a good deal of material. It could easily use up the best part of a metre of 90 cm-wide fabric.

LENGTHENING A FLARED SKIRT WITH A HIP-YOKE

A flared skirt can usually be lengthened more successfully from the waist than at the hem. A hip-yoke, straight or shaped, could give new fashion interest to an old skirt. But make sure first that the darts, and the side and back seam turnings, are wide enough to allow the skirt to settle 6–7 cm lower on the hips.

1 Unpick the waist finish, and take out the zip.
2 Using the unaltered skirt as a guide, cut paper patterns of its waist-line, back and front, and down about 10 cm towards the hips (figure 3.11a). Disregarding any darts or other seams, draw the pattern in one piece, from side seam to side seam. Add turnings of 1.5 cm along waist and side edges, and a straight-grain arrow (figure 3.11b).

Figure 3.11

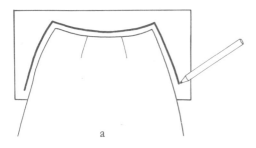
a

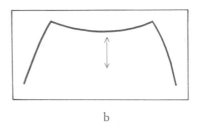
b

3 To complete the pattern, draw in the depth of the yoke, and the shaping of its lower edge. This may be designed to fit in with skirt seams, or existing seamline pockets (figure 3.12). Or new pocket flaps could be incorporated in the yoke seam, to emphasize the line (figure 3.13). When drawing in the lower edge of the yoke, allow for a turning of 1.5 cm.

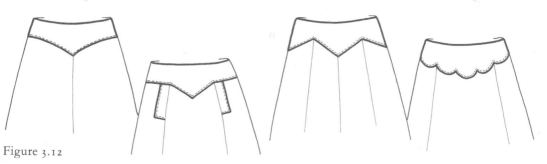
Figure 3.12

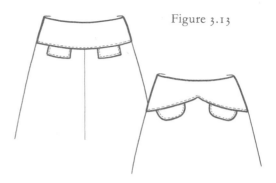

Figure 3.13

4 Unpick any darts, so that the skirt can lie lower on the hips. Unpick the top few centimetres of the side seams. Press.

5 Yokes look better top-stitched in place. So fold under the turning along the lower edge of the yoke, clipping corners or curves so that the fold will lie flat (figure 3.14). Press.

Figure 3.14

Figure 3.15

6 With right sides uppermost, pin the front yoke over the front skirt, dropping the skirt as far as possible. Repeat for the back of the skirt (figure 3.15).

7 Pin up the side seams. Try on to check the balance of the skirt. The yoke should be re-pinned until you are satisfied with the way the skirt hangs.

8 Top-stitch the yoke sections to the skirt sections, using buttonhole twist and setting the longest stitch the machine will make.

9 Stitch the side seams, and reset the zip. (See page 50.)

10 Replace the waistband with a petersham ribbon, as shown on page 34.

FLOUNCES

This easy method is equally suitable for bringing an ankle-length skirt down to floor level; or for lengthening a child's dress – with or without a matching waistband (figure 3.16).

A flounce will need to be at least half as wide again as the skirt. Allow 3–4 cm depth for a hem, and 1.5 cm for a seam turning at the upper edge. Flounces may be cut along the straight grain or, for a softer line, on the true cross of the fabric.

1 Unpick the skirt hem and press it out.

2 Seam together the ends of the flounce sections. Turn up and finish its hem.

Figure 3.16

3 To gather the flounce to fit, set your machine at its longest stitch, and slightly loosen the tension on the needle thread. Stitch all round the upper edge of the flounce; first 1 cm, and then again 2 cm, from the edge. There is less strain on the gathering threads, and they are easier to draw up, if the machining is done in several sections (figure 3.17).

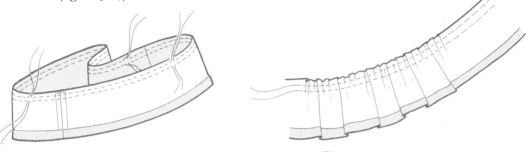

Figure 3.17   Figure 3.18

4 Holding the wrong-side thread ends (the bobbin thread on the machine), draw up both together until the flounce fits the skirt. Make sure that the fullness is evenly distributed (figure 3.18).
5 Pin the flounce to the skirt, right sides together and raw edges matching. If the pins are placed at right angles to the edge, you can with care machine straight over them. Stitch midway between the two gathering threads (figure 3.19).
6 Neaten the raw edges of flounce and skirt together, by zigzag machining.
7 Pull out the gathering thread that shows on the right side.
    There is an even simpler method of flouncing – suitable particularly for children's dresses or for sleeve or neckline finishes. Cut the flounce twice the finished depth, plus 3 cm. Join the sections end-to-end. Fold the whole flounce lengthways, right side out, with raw edges matching (figure 3.20). Gather through both layers together, and stitch to the skirt. In this way, you will not even have to work a hem.

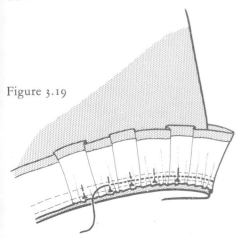

Figure 3.19

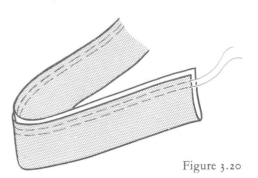

Figure 3.20

Shortening Most shortening is perfectly straightforward, consisting simply of taking up a deeper hem. But even here there are one or two special cases.

SHORTENING A FLARED SKIRT

If a flared skirt is shortened at the hem, its proportions may look skimpy. It is much better to shorten from the waist, so keeping the full flare at the hemline. The only problem is the resetting of the zip.

1 Unpick and take off the waistband complete. This can be used again.
2 Unpick the zip from the skirt.
3 Trim from the waistline the amount by which the skirt is to be shortened (figure 3.21).
4 Open up the top 10 cm of all the skirt seams. They will need to be reshaped in to the waist, by pinning very slightly wider seam turnings. Pin on the waistband and try on the skirt. Make sure that it not only fits, but also hangs level.
5 The zip will need to be placed lower in its seam than before. Stitch a new, firm upper end to this seam, and reset the zip. (See page 50.)
6 Stitch the remaining seams up to the waistline.
7 Re-set the waistband, in the same way as it was originally.

Figure 3.21

SHORTENING A PLEATED SKIRT

Here, you may have a dilemma. If the pleats are taken right up to the waistline, any alteration there may be awkward. On the other hand, if the skirt is of polyester, or any man-made fibre in which the pleats are heat-set during manufacture, it may be difficult to shorten at the hem. You may not be able to press in a new reverse crease to the hem-turnings of the pleats, without using so much heat that you risk damaging the surface of the fabric. These are the alternative methods you could try.

To shorten from the waist follow the same steps as for shortening a flared skirt. Safe seams to take in, to shape the waistline, are those which do not include the upper ends of pleats.

To shorten at the hemline

1 Cut off the old hem along its crease. (One's instinct is against trimming off any fabric anywhere; but here it is best to get rid of the excess.)
2 Decide the depth of the new hem; in a pleated skirt, 3–4 cm should be enough. Press out the old pleat creases below the new hemline. On woollen fabrics, press through a damp cloth. On man-made fibres the cloth must be dry. Never press directly on the fabric itself.
3 Now press up the new hem turning. Baste this in place, to hold firmly both the fold and the free edge (figure 3.22).
4 Finish the hem by catch-stitching, as shown on page 19.
5 Baste the pleat edges back in place and press again, going over the crease of each pleat separately (figure 3.23).
6 The inner fold of a pleat may be edge-stitched by machine, to hold its shape at the hem (figure 3.24).

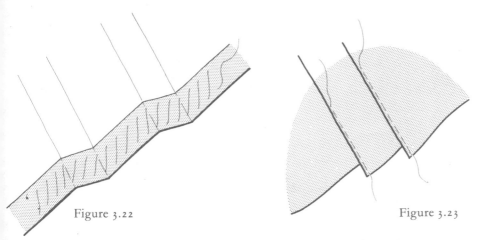

Figure 3.22

Figure 3.23

7 If there is a seam at the inside of a pleat, it may have been stitched after the hem was worked. If so, use the same method with the new hem (figure 3.25).

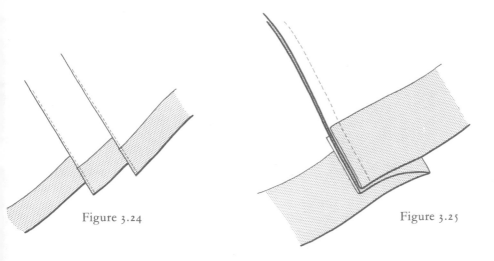

Figure 3.24

Figure 3.25

SHORTENING A DRESS FOR A YOUNGER SISTER

Ideally, children's clothes should in the first place be made to allow for growth. So if you are shortening an older girl's dress to pass on to a younger, make sure that any alterations can be easily reversed later on. Use a stitch long enough to make future unpicking practicable without a magnifying-glass. Never cut away any material; leave it in wider seams or a deeper hem.

A child's dress which is too long may also present other problems; too much width in the bodice, and also perhaps too much depth in the armhole. Unless these fitting faults are very obvious, they are better left alone; just rely on a belt to give shape.

But in extreme cases, length, width and armhole depth can all be dealt with together, as shown in figure 3.26:

Figure 3.26

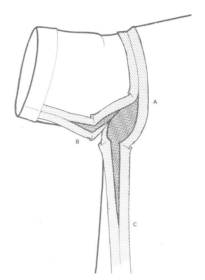

1 Unpick the *armhole seams* for 5 cm on each side of the underarm seams (A).
2 Unpick 5 cm of the *sleeve seams*, from the armholes downwards (B).
3 Unpick the *side seams* of the bodice, from the armholes to below the waistline (C).
4 Press out all the turnings of the unpicked seams.
5 Pin the sleeve seams and the bodice side seams with slightly wider turnings than before, and re-stitch. Do not take in more than is absolutely necessary, as children grow so quickly and you might have to let it out again all the sooner.
6 Re-stitch round the lower part of the armholes, matching together the two newly-altered seams. Do not trim away any of the turnings below the armholes, but press open all the seams.
7 On the bodice, mark the natural waistline with tailor's chalk or tacking.
8 With the dress inside out, stitch a new waist seam along the marked line, taking in an equal amount from the skirt – in effect, making a pleat round the waistline. You will fit the dress better by shortening it in this way, rather than by just turning up the hem (figure 3.27).

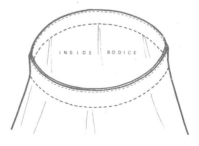

Figure 3.27

9 Do not unpick the old waist seam; the extra fabric will lie quite flat if pressed up towards the bodice. Thus the dress can be let down again later with the minimum of trouble.

LETTING OUT A TIGHT DRESS

In well-made, good-quality dresses, it is surprising how much spare fabric there is in seam turnings. In cheaper clothes, there may be little or nothing. But usually, with very minor alterations, one can enlarge a dress by at least one size.

1 Unpick the side seams from 3 cm below the armhole, right down to a few cm above the hem. It is better not to tamper with the armhole itself, as this adds unnecessary complications. Equally, it is unwise to make the alteration at the waistline only; the new seamline must be continued right down the skirt, to give a smooth line over the hips.

2 Press out the seam-turnings flat, and if they are not already over-locked, secure the edges at once by zigzag machining over the edge – or, if your machine has only a straight stitch, by hand-overcasting (figure 3.28). It is essential to protect these edges from fraying, as you will be working with very narrow turnings.

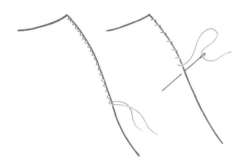

Figure 3.28

3 Now tack up the seams again, 5 mm from their edges, tapering to meet the old seamline at each end. Try on, and check the size. If the seam originally had 1.5 cm turnings, the two edges will give an extra 2 cm of width – both side seams giving a total of 4 cm, very nearly a whole size. But in most well-made or model garments, the original seam allowance will have been wider than 1.5 cm – so one can reckon on this simple alteration giving a full extra size to the garment, making for instance a Size 12 up to a Size 14 (figure 3.29).

4 This is only the beginning. Bust darts and back-waist darts may also be let out. One will lose a certain amount of under-bust shaping, of course; and it may be that there are no corresponding darts in the skirt and skirt lining that can also be let out. If the tightness is above the waist, there is no problem. But if the waistline itself is to be enlarged, then the upper edge of the skirt must be let out too. The best solution is to raise the skirt about 2 cm; as skirts are cut

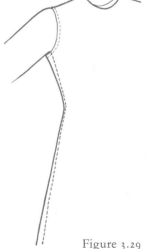

Figure 3.29

*2 (opposite) A dress
altered into a pinafore
dress (see page 61)*

narrower towards the waist, any raising will automatically give extra ease (figure 3.30).

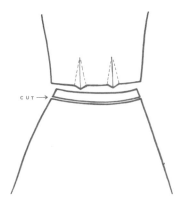

Figure 3.30

If you are altering only the front darts, it may be necessary to alter only the front of the skirt. For instance, on a fully flared evening skirt, lifting it along the front of the waistline by 2 cm will not affect its drape. But for a larger alteration, or on a more fitted skirt, it would be better to lift the skirt 2 cm all round, also letting out the back-waist darts of the bodice. This will mean that the skirt will hang properly level; it will also mean resetting the lower end of a back zip. However, it is worth while taking this trouble, as the result can transform an impossibly tight, unwearable dress into one with plenty of room to hang well. The author (averse to dieting), satisfactorily altered a model dress from Size 12 to Size 16 in this way. (See illustration 1, page 6.)

5 It is also possible to gain extra back width between the shoulders by resetting a back zip with narrower turnings. This is a last resort. For one thing, it may affect the fit of the neckline. For another, the stitching of the zip may have pulled the fabric slightly, and the unpicked seam may leave permanent marks down each side of the new zip placing.

LETTING OUT A SKIRT

Here, the problem is much easier. There is usually plenty of fabric in skirt seams, and normally at least three seams to play with.

If the alteration is simply to let out the waistline, these are the steps:

1 Take off the waistband completely, and unpick all its stitching.

2 Unpick the waistline darts, press and re-pin, letting them out evenly all round. It should be possible to release 1 cm of fabric from each dart, giving a good 4 cm extra width. As the new darts will be narrower, they could probably be made shorter at the same time. Make sure that they are pinned along the same centre-line, and that the new stitching tapers finely to the point of each dart (figure 3.31).

3 If you also need to alter the side seams, then both must be let out equally. Taper the alteration back into the existing seam at hip level, about 20–25 cm down from the waist (figure 3.32).

Figure 3.31

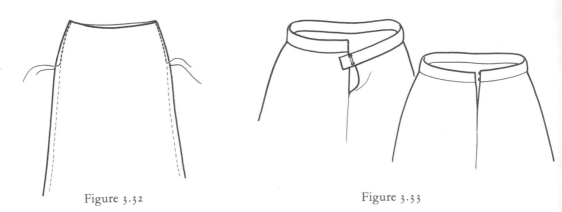

Figure 3.32   Figure 3.33

4 A skirt let out at one side only will never hang well, so where there
   is a side zip it is better to let out the back seam instead. As this will
   usually be on the straight grain of the fabric, the alteration should
   be taken right down the length of the skirt, including the hem,
   without any tapering.

5 The skirt lining must now be let out by the same amount. As lining
   is so important to the hang of a garment, you may decide to replace
   it with a new lining. Use the old one as a pattern, allowing for the
   dart and seam alterations.

6 The waistband will now be too short. If there was the usual 5 cm
   hook-and-eye underlap, this can be used as an extension, giving an
   edge-to-edge finish (figure 3.33). If, however, there is nothing to
   spare, you could let in a small piece of matching fabric to the centre
   back or side. Allow this piece to be 6 cm longer than its finished
   measurement, to allow for turnings on the two seams (figure 3.34).
   It may on the other hand be neater to mount the skirt on a petersham ribbon – the stiff polyester ones are best. It will lie invisibly
   inside the waistline. Neaten the raw edge of the skirt on to the
   petersham with zigzag machining or binding (figure 3.35).

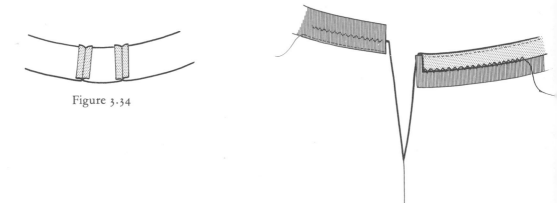

Figure 3.34

Figure 3.35

If the alteration is to the hipline only, it is far simpler. Just unpick the available seams from 3 cm below the waist, down to just above hem level. Tack, try on and re-stitch as necessary, always tapering side seam alterations to nothing just above the hem. Alter the lining in the same way.

TAKING IN A DRESS

Taking In

The critical measurement of a dress is the width across the back, between the shoulders. If the garment is very much too wide here, it cannot be made to fit properly without unpicking it completely, and remodelling. The neckline would have to be taken in, at the centre-back seam or by neckline darts; the collar and facings would need to be re-cut; and the sleeves reset into altered armholes. You would have a major operation on your hands.

But if a dress once fitted you, it will not need such drastic treatment. Even if you have lost a good deal of weight, the basic measurements across the shoulders and round the neckline will not be affected, because they correspond to actual bone structure. It is much more likely that the measurements of bust, waist or hips will have changed. In that case, the alterations needed are quite simple, and do not entail taking the entire garment to pieces. It follows that if you are tempted by a sales bargain in too large a size, you should look very carefully at the fit across the back. If this is satisfactory, the alterations to the rest of the garment will be straightforward: if not, you may not have a bargain.

If there is a waist seam

1 Unpick the skirt from the bodice, releasing the lower end of any zip, so that you can handle bodice and skirt separately. This makes sewing easier, and saves time.

2 Unpick the side seams of the bodice (to within 5 cm of the armhole), and the side seams of the skirt.

3 Pin the seams up again, taking more fabric into the turnings. Taper the new skirt seamline right down to the hem.

4 Do not unpick the bodice and skirt darts but, keeping to their original line, pin them wider and a fraction longer (figure 3.36).

5 Any size alteration should be spread between all the available darts and seams; several small alterations give better shape than a few large ones. Each dart and seam can be taken in a maximum of 1 cm on each edge. Thus, with four darts and two side seams, one could reduce the waist measurement, for instance, by as much as 12 cm – more than two sizes. This is, of course, a far larger size change than normally needed.

6 Try on the bodice for fit. Stitch the altered side seams and darts.

7 Stitch the darts and side seams of the skirt.

8 Pin bodice and skirt together, and try on again, to check the hang of the skirt.

9 Lastly, stitch the bodice to the skirt, and reset the end of the zip.

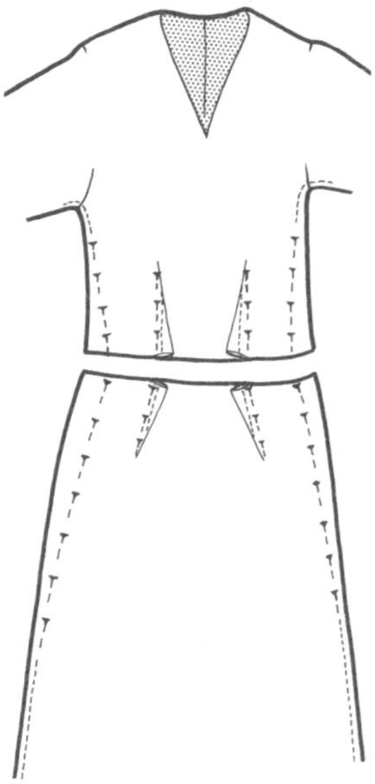

If there is no waist seam   Treat the darts and seams in just the same way,

Figure 3.36

but to avoid puckering, they should be snipped across at the waistline. After pressing, they will open out a little, and the dress will hang smoothly (figure 3.37).

Figure 3.37

TAKING IN A SKIRT

This is simply the reverse of letting out a skirt. (See page 32.)

For a smaller waist   Take off the waistband completely. Do not shorten it; keep the extra length as an underlap – an insurance against putting on weight again. Take in the available darts and seams equally; but leave the zip in place. Reset the waistband, making the underlap on the back edge of the zip opening.

For smaller hips   If there is to be no change at the waist, alter the side seams only of the skirt and lining. The waist finish can be left intact. Taper the new seamline to meet the old one just above hem level.

TAKING IN A DRESS FOR A STOOPED FIGURE

Older people, because of a more curved posture of the backbone or shoulders, sometimes find their clothes too ample in front, yet needing extra shaping at the back. The collar is likely to stand away from the neck at centre-back, and folds of fabric tend to form at the sides and front of the waistline. There is usually plenty of length from shoulder to waist, even at the back; it is the distribution of this length that sets the problem (figure 3.38). This is a slightly more elaborate alteration, but well worth making to correct the hang of a good dress. It can be done without disturbing the collar, neckline or sleeves.

1 Unpick the waist seam, and release the lower end of any zip.
2 Unpick the side seams of the bodice to within 5 cm of the armholes.
3 On the bodice back, pin darts just below the armhole. This fitting must be done on the figure, so the help of a friend is needed (figure 3.39).
4 Pin the side seams together again. Because of the new dart, the front edge of the seam will extend below the back edge. Leave this extra length for the moment.
5 If more shaping is needed to the upper part of the back, a dart can be made in each shoulder seam. To do this, unpick 5 or 6 cm along the middle of the seam; do not touch its armhole or neck ends. On

Figure 3.38

Figure 3.39

the back shoulder edge, pin a dart wide enough to bring the back neckline closer in to the neck (figure 3.40). This should be a short dart, not taking away any width from between the shoulder blades. If there is already a dart in this position, widen it until the neckline fit is improved.

Figure 3.40

6 Make a corresponding dart of equal width in front of the shoulder seam, in order to bring both edges back to the same length. The front dart should be long – perhaps 20 cm – to reduce the front full-ness caused by round shoulders. It can be taken down almost to the point of the bust (figure 3.41).
7 Slip-baste the darts, back and front, as shown on page 15, and stitch them. Stitch the shoulder seams.
8 Stitch the bodice side seams.
9 Try on the bodice again. If the front is too full at the waistline, pin under-bust darts.
10 Now mark with pins the natural level of the waistline across the front. The bodice will almost certainly be too long at the centre-front; you will also need to mark the side seams a little higher, because of the side-back darts (figure 3.42).

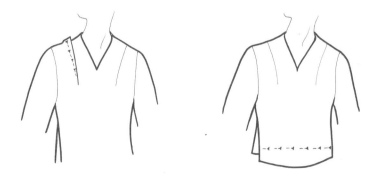

Figure 3.41   Figure 3.42

11 Pin the skirt in place along the new waistline. Make sure that it hangs level when seen from the side. If it tilts forward, drop the skirt a little on the front of the bodice; if it tilts towards the back, raise it on the bodice (figure 3.43). Do not alter the *skirt* waistline; make any alterations on the bodice.

12 Stitch the waist seam, and reset the lower end of the zip.

Figure 3.43

3 (Opposite) An over-sweater made from a knitted suit (see page 66)

4 Simply Updating

The details of style that may make an old dress unwearable are often relatively easy to alter. Given the current neckline, edgings, fastenings or trim, a garment may take on quite a new fashion life.

The Neckline This is the most noticeable feature of a dress, so be bold in its treatment. Think not only of a new collar – though that in itself can work wonders – but of the whole cut of the neckline. Contrasting fabric can be helpful here, supported perhaps by decorative top-stitching.

STYLES

Collar shapes vary from season to season to such an extent that it would be useless to give actual patterns. These can be drafted as you wish, following the instructions on page 114. But remember that a collar need not be set on the standard round neckline. A bodice with a shirt-collar and front buttoning, for instance, could be given a square or V neck, with a lower-cut collar (figure 4.1).

If you are making a low neckline, mark it with pins before cutting down into the bodice. However low the scoop or square, keep the line close to the sides of the neck. When you cut, remember to leave turnings of 1.5 cm all round. You could finish this type of neckline with an inside facing, as shown on page 62, or with binding (figure 4.2).

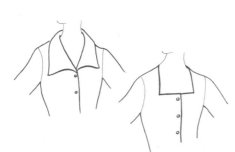

Figure 4.1

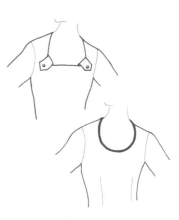

Figure 4.2

A new, narrower collar could also be made from an old one. For instance, a straight-cut shirt collar could be converted into a stand-up band or mandarin collar.

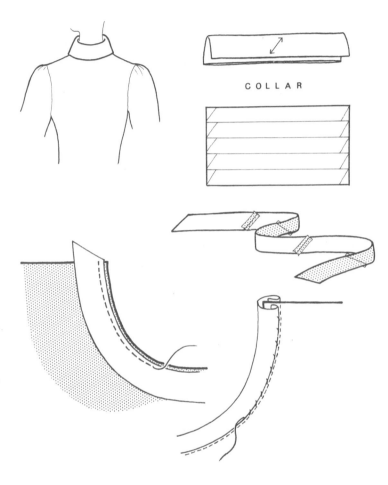

C O L L A R

Figure 4.3

THE OLD COLLAR

This may be useful in providing matching fabric. A roll collar cut on the cross is almost ready-made for use as binding; it will yield four or five times its own length in bias strips 3–4 cm wide, which could be used to finish any new shape at the neckline. The strips are joined along the straight thread, as shown; machined to the right side of the garment; then turned in on the wrong side and hemmed in place (figure 4.3). Or else the bias strips could be made into rouleau ties to fasten a neck opening. Here is the method. A bias strip 4 cm wide is folded down its length, right side inside, and machined along the *centre*. (This gives a firm, fat rouleau; if you were to machine near the raw edges, the rouleau would come out flat and limp.) Use a small machine stitch, to give stretch to the rouleau. Turn it right-side-out by threading through with a safety-pin (figure 4.4).

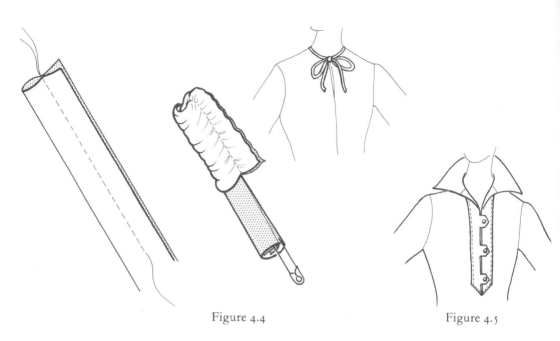

Figure 4.4   Figure 4.5

USING CONTRAST

An entirely different neckline can be achieved with contrasting facings, applied to the right side of the garment. You could retain the old shape, or re-cut it; in either case, the facing would emphasize the line. It could also be combined with a new collar (figure 4.5).

USING THE SLEEVES

If you do not want contrast, you could convert the dress to a sleeveless style, and use the sleeve fabric for a collar and facings. You would also need to make armhole facings, or finish the armholes with binding.

SETTING ON A COLLAR

With facings   For facings and collar patterns, see pages 113 and 114.
1   Make up the collar, trim the turnings, turn to the right side, and press. Top-stitch if liked.
2   Pin the collar in place, clipping the neck edge of the bodice round the curve (figure 4.6).

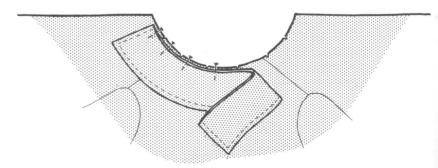

Figure 4.6

3 Cut neckline facings. Seam them together at the shoulders.
4 Lay the facings, wrong side up, over the collar and bodice, matching at the shoulder seams. Tack through all thicknesses, and stitch
   (figure 4.7).

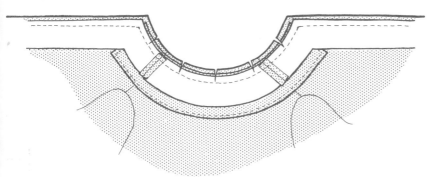

Figure 4.7

5 Trim the turnings to different widths, to get rid of unnecessary
   bulk. Round curves, clip at right angles to the stitching, so that the
   seam can lie flat. Turn the facings to the inside, and press. Catch
   down at the shoulder seams.

Without facings
1 Tack the underneath layer of the collar to the neckline, and stitch.
   Press the turnings upwards inside the collar.
2 Fold in the seam allowance of the upper layer of collar, clip as
   necessary, and fell round the inside of the neck, just above the line
   of stitching (figure 4.8).

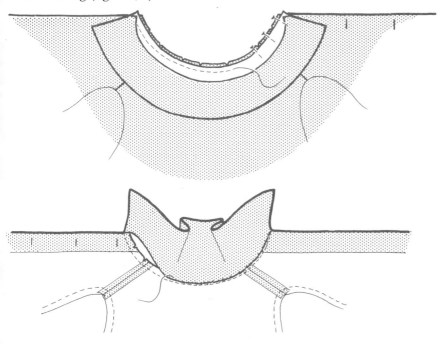

Figure 4.8

Sleeves If you have to replace sleeves, do not despair. Taken step by step, they are not difficult to set in.

1 Unpick the old sleeve from its armhole, keeping all turnings intact. Unpick the sleeve underarm seam, press, and use the old sleeve as a pattern for the new ones.

2 Place the new sleeves side by side, to be sure you make them up as a pair. With reversible fabric, it is all too easy to make both for the same side of the body. (The front armhole edge of the sleeve is cut in a deeper curve than the back. It will also be marked with a single notch on the pattern, whereas the back edge will have a double notch.) Stitch the sleeve seams (figure 4.9).

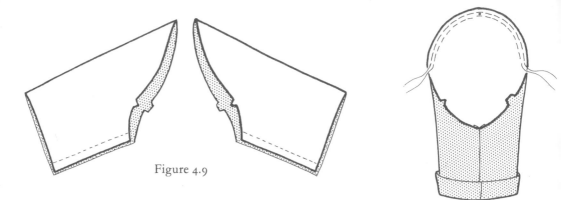

Figure 4.9

Figure 4.10

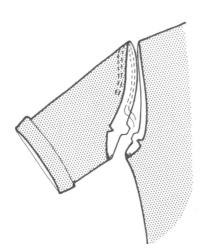

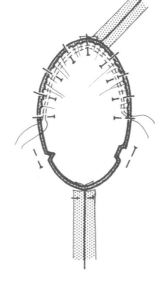

Figure 4.11   Figure 4.12   Figure 4.13

3 Finish the lower end of the sleeve. This is simpler when you can handle the sleeve by itself, rather than when it trails the rest of the garment along with it.
4 Gather the upper half of the sleevehead, and draw up the thread a little (figure 4.10).
5 Match the sleeve to its armhole, right sides out (figure 4.11).
6 Turn the bodice wrong side out over the sleeve; pin together at the underarm seams and at the front and back notches (figure 4.12).
7 Pin the centre of the sleevehead to the shoulder seam of the bodice. Pull up the gathering threads so that the sleeve fits the armhole. Distribute the gathers evenly on each side, and pin as shown (also figure 4.12).
8 Tack all round the armhole, 1.5 cm from the raw edges. Try on to be sure of the line.
9 Machine where you have tacked.
10 Trim, and neaten the raw edges with zigzag machining (figure 4.13).

Edgings and Facings

A suit can often be brought up to date by altering the cut of the fronts, or the levels and spacing of the buttonholes. There is no need, even, to retain the overlap at the front edges. A double-breasted jacket could be re-styled as a single-breasted one, or the fronts could be cut back and finished edge-to-edge. If old buttonholes need to be covered up, draw together their two sides with stitches alternately over each edge, before applying a right-side facing (figure 4.14).

Figure 4.14

FACINGS

Front facings can be turned either to the inside or to the outside of a garment. Both kinds are cut to fit the garment edge. See the instructions on page 113 for making patterns of facings.

Right-side facings, which can be in a contrasting fabric, will become an important feature of the style. They can enliven the look of a suit, and may alter its proportions by giving the effect of a stripe down the centre-front. This could be an attractive and slimming detail. As the width and shape of the facings are so important, it is best to try them out first in brown paper, pinned in place to see how they look. The inner edge of the facing may be shaped to any line that will accentuate or give interest to the design. Figure 4.15 gives one example. First, turn under and press the turnings along the inner edge of the facing, clipping or mitring corners (figure 4.16). Apply the facing with its right side to the wrong side of the garment. Tack and stitch the seam. Trim the turnings into layers, clip curves, and cut across corners to get rid of bulk. Turn the facing over to the right side, so that the seam-line is just out of sight behind the edge of the garment, and press. Top-stitch 3 mm from the fold of the free edge (figure 4.17).

Figure 4.15

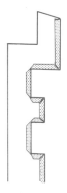

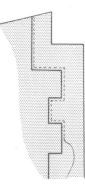

Figure 4.16

Inside facings   Place the garment and facing right sides together, tack and stitch. Turn the facing to the inside and press, so that the seamline falls just inside the finished edge. The facing of a jacket is folded in after the hemline has been tacked up (figure 4.18).

BRAID
This useful trim can be applied just to the right side, top-stitched along both its edges. Or it can be bought ready-folded, so that it encloses the edge of the garment – useful where a worn edge needs camouflage. Place the wider 'half' of the braid under the garment edge, and top-stitch from the right side, through all the thicknesses (figure 4.19). Braid looks best if taken not only down the fronts, but also round the hem. Consider using it on pocket flaps, too, to pull the design together. Mitre the braid at corners, or ease it round curves with gathering threads (figure 4.20). Ready-made knitted trim can be used effectively in the same way as braid.

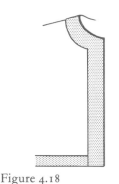

Figure 4.17

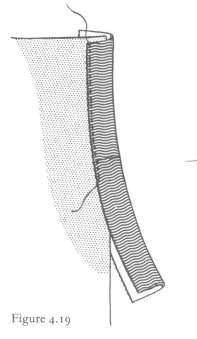

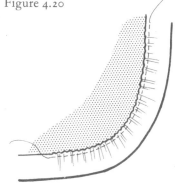

Figure 4.18

Figure 4.19

Figure 4.20

BINDING

On heavier garments, you could consider a binding of soft, fine leather or suède, cut in strips 4 cm wide. With right sides together, stitch it to the garment edge. Then turn the binding over to the inside, and top-stitch from the *right* side, using a zipper-foot on the machine (see page 50), so that you can sew right into the channel formed by the first seam. The top-stitching should then be quite invisible (figure 4.21).

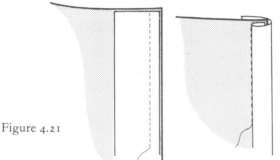

Figure 4.21

Leather is not easy to manoeuvre round curves, but can be mitred at corners. Gentle tapping with a hammer will settle it in place.

Fastenings

New fastenings to a dress or jacket should be planned along with any new treatment of the front edges. A right-side facing, for instance, can incorporate buttonholes, or braided edges can be fastened with a zip.

MACHINE-MADE BUTTONHOLES

If your machine has an automatic buttonholer, then follow the instruction booklet. But you can make equally good buttonholes with any swing-needle machine, provided that the needle can be set into a left-hand position. The following method is fool-proof.

1 Buttonholes are always worked through a double thickness of fabric. Through both thicknesses, mark with tacking the inner and outer ends of the buttonholes. Pencil in the line of each one (figure 4.22).
2 Set the stitch *width* to a little less than half the maximum. Set the stitch *length* short enough to make a close satin stitch.
3 Slightly loosen the tension on the needle thread. Move the needle to the left-hand position. The next steps can be followed through figure 4.23.

Figure 4.22

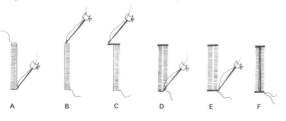

A   B   C   D   E   F

Figure 4.23

4 Begin at the inner end of a buttonhole. Work down the left-hand side of the marking – A.

5 When you reach the outer end, leave the needle down after it has swung to the right. Raise the presser foot, and pivot the work round on the needle, so that you are in position to work the second side of the buttonhole. Lower the presser-foot – B.

6 First raise the needle out of the work; then set the stitch-width to maximum.

7 Work 6–8 wide stitches across the end of the buttonhole. Hold the fabric firmly in place, so that these stitches all come on top of each other; do not let the work travel through the machine. End with the needle up – C.

8 Reset the stitch-width again, to slightly less than half the maximum, and work the second side of the buttonhole. Be sure that the stitches do not interlock with those down the first side – there should be a clear thread of fabric between them – D.

9 Repeat steps 6 and 7 to finish the other end of the buttonhole – E.

10 Cut open the buttonhole with a seam-ripper, working (for safety) from ends to middle – F.

11 Pull thread ends to the inside, knot them and thread them away between the two thicknesses of fabric.

STRAP FASTENINGS

Buttonholes can be worked on a strap, before applying it to the garment. (A safety precaution for the nervous: if the buttonhole turns out to be a disaster, you could discard the strap and make another.) Strap fastenings could be an attractive detail on informal outdoor clothes, perhaps using toggles instead of buttons. Alternatively, the straps could be fastened with buckles (figure 4.24).

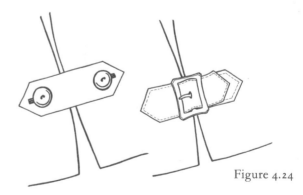

Figure 4.24

LOOP BUTTONHOLES

These are made from rouleaux – see page 41. The loops are tacked to the right side of the garment edge, turned inwards away from the edge. Then the front facing is tacked in place over the loops, and the seam is stitched. When the facing is folded to the inside, the loops will turn outwards along the edge of the garment (figure 4.25).

4 (Opposite) A skirt made from a flared coat (see page 72)

Figure 4.25

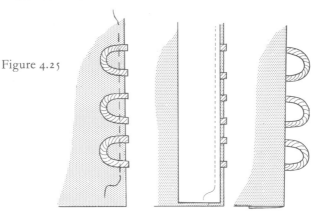

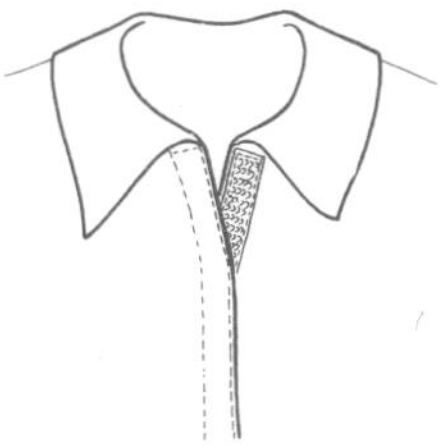

VELCRO

This fastening is simply a pair of tapes, pressed together. The surface of one tape is covered with minute nylon hooks, and the surface of the other with a soft nylon fuzz. The soft tape is stitched to the overlap edge, and the hooked tape to the underlap. Velcro is particularly useful for children's and sports clothing. When machine-stitched in place along both edges of the tapes, all that is visible on the outside of the garment is a double row of top-stitching (figure 4.26).

Figure 4.26

ZIPS

To set in a zip by machine, you will need to use a special zipper-foot on the machine. This has only one toe, which can be set at either side of the needle, allowing stitches to be made close up to a zip or to piping cord (figure 4.27).

Setting a Zip into a Seam Avoid the serpentine look, mark of the amateur. Here is an infallible method:

Figure 4.27

1 Set a long back zip if possible *before* stitching the side seams. You can then work on the flat, not through a tunnel of garment. (Set on a collar, too, *after* the zip is in.)
2 Stitch the seam from the lower end of the zip down to the hem.
3 Now machine-baste the zip opening, taking up turnings the same width as for the seam. Machine-basting is simply machining with the longest possible stitch, so that the threads can be pulled out easily (figure 4.28).
4 Press open the turnings of seam and zip placing.
5 Lay the zip in place under the basted opening. Working from the right side of the garment, pin the zip at 3 cm intervals, from the top downwards. You will be able to feel the line of the zip through the fabric; keep it centred under the seam. If you pin accurately now, the zip will come out with evenly matched turnings.
6 Baste in place through all the thicknesses. Take out the pins (figure 4.29).
7 On the wrong side, machine along the centre of the zipper tape, down one side, across the stop-end, and up the other side. Make the turns by pivoting the work round on the needle (figure 4.30).
8 Remove the basting and machine-basting.

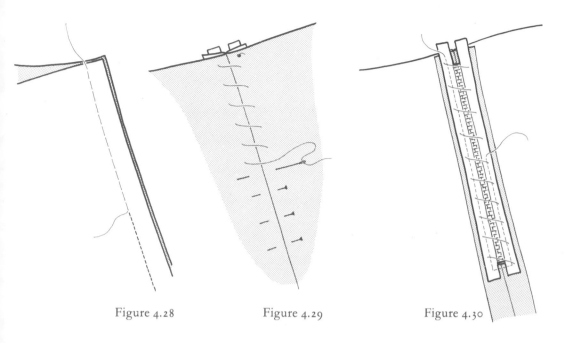

Figure 4.28   Figure 4.29   Figure 4.30

Setting a Zip into a Slot   Even without a centre-front seam, a bodice can be given a front zip to set off a collar. In this type of opening, the zipper tapes cannot be invisible; but a virtue may be made of this, by repeating down the zip any colour contrast you plan at the neckline.

1   Cut the opening the length of the zip, making a V cut at the lower end. Fold under 6–10 mm turnings along the sides and at the end.
2   Tack the zip in place behind the opening.
3   Top-stitch 3 mm from the folds (figure 4.31).

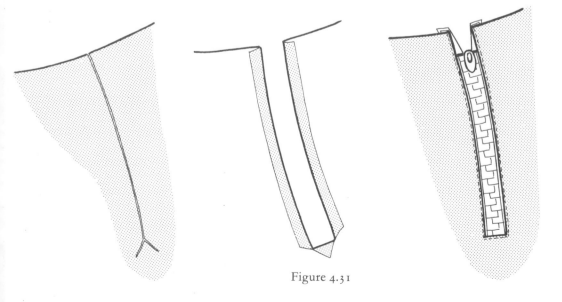

Figure 4.31

BELTS

To keep its shape, a belt must be built on a firm foundation. Use polyester petersham ribbon, which will resist creasing. Figure 4.32 shows the steps.

Figure 4.32

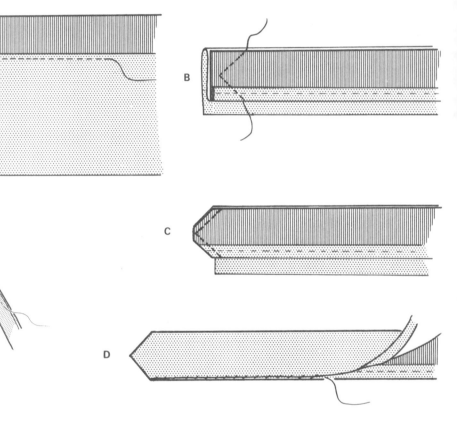

1 Cut the covering fabric $2\frac{1}{2}$ times the width of the petersham. Machine stitch as shown, with the right side of the fabric upwards – A.

2 Fold the fabric up behind the petersham; fold again level with the top edge, and let the fabric extend below the petersham. Stitch the pointed end – B.

3 Trim across the end – C.

4 Turn the point through to the right side. Turn in the free edge of the fabric, and fell along the length of the belt, just inside the lower edge, pulling the fabric taut round the petersham as you stitch – D.

Belt Carriers Each carrier will need to be twice as long as the belt width, to allow for turnings and for ease round the belt. Cut a strip of the dress fabric 3 cm wide, and long enough to make all the carriers needed. Fold the strip edges-to-middle, fold again, and machine (figure 4.32a). Cut into the separate carriers. Sew the belt carriers in place at the side seams. Back-stitching by hand is easier than machining (figure 4.32b).

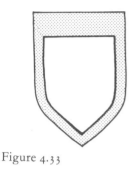

Figure 4.33

Figure 4.34

Of all the many kinds of pocket – those with flaps or welts, those in **Pockets** slots or seams – the most conspicuous and adaptable are perhaps patch pockets. They are also the simplest to apply. As they can be added to a finished garment, one can more clearly judge the final effect before cutting out the pockets. Needless to say, one should first experiment with pinned-on paper shapes; quite a small change in their size may make all the difference to the line of the whole garment.

1   Cut a paper pattern the size of the finished pocket.
2   Fold the garment with its left and right fronts together. Using the pattern, mark with tailor's tacks (see page 16) through both sides. This ensures that the pockets will be exactly level and even. The placings of the two top corners only need to be marked.
3   Cut a piece of tape 3 cm longer than the pocket mouth, and tack it to the wrong side of the garment, behind the top of the pocket placing. It will support the fabric and prevent tearing or pulling.
4   Cut the pockets from the paper pattern, allowing turnings of 1.5 cm at the sides and bottom, and 4 cm along the top edge (figure 4.33).
5   Strengthen the top 4 cm with a strip of light-weight fusible interfacing, such as Vilene, ironed to the wrong side. Neaten the edge with zigzag machining (figure 4.34).
6   Fold the top turning over to the right side, to form a facing, and stitch 1.5 cm in from the edge, all round the sides and bottom of the pocket (figure 4.35).
7   Trim off the interfacing in the seam turnings. Notch the turnings at curves, and trim diagonally at corners.
8   Turn the facing through to the wrong side, and press. Press the remaining turnings to the wrong side, so that the stitching is just out of sight (figure 4.36).
9   Tack the pockets in place, and top-stitch round the sides and bottom, starting and finishing with little triangles of stitching. Pull the thread ends through to the wrong side, and tie off (figure 4.37).

Figure 4.35

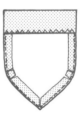

Figure 4.36

Figure 4.37

Covering Disasters A small tear or cigarette burn in a garment need not mean the end of its useful life. There are several ways of covering up – but the old-fashioned patch and the apologetic darn are not among them. Try to hide the damage by bringing in a new detail of style, and making a feature of it.

POCKETS

If the tear is in a position where you could possibly apply a pocket, this would be a good solution to the problem.

BRAID

Cover the tear with two or three rows of narrow braid, or with lace. This should be taken right across the front, or right round the dress; it could even be repeated on collar or sleeve to pull the design together.

MACHINE EMBROIDERY

On thin fabric, tack a small matching piece behind the hole. Then use your machine's widest and most elaborate stitches as camouflage, perhaps in several rows, as above. On the wrong side, trim off the raw edges of the patch.

MOTIFS

For children's clothes, where accidents are more frequent, an embroidered motif could be stitched on; again, this may be more effective if a scatter of several motifs is used. On such garments as jeans or anoraks, there is no problem – simply apply a bright patch, preferably of bizarre shape. This could be sewn on with machine satin-stitch, in a contrasting colour for further impact.

DARNING CHECKED TWEED

This is possibly the only fabric in which a darn can be invisible. It would certainly show on a plain or smooth fabric, and would serve only to draw the eye.

1 Trim any loose ends of thread from the hole.
2 Use warp threads from the seam turnings, and weft threads from the hem, in a blunt-pointed tapestry needle. Use a separate thread for each strand; do not double-back, as in ordinary darning.
3 Begin 1 cm away from the hole, in sound fabric. At the left side of the hole, darn in the first vertical (warp) thread, next to the last unbroken one. Leave a short length of thread at each end, on the wrong side. Lay down all the warp threads in turn, from left to right, keeping to the exact pattern of the check in colour and weave.
4 Next, lay down the weft threads, weaving in the pattern as you go.
5 On the wrong side, the darn will look like figure 4.38. The new threads (shaded) are woven in with the trimmed ends of the old.
6 Gently pull up the lengths of new thread at each side of the darn, to tighten it. Trim off the loose ends 3 mm from the fabric.
7 Press under a damp cloth.

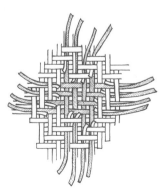

Figure 4.38

5 Turning and Relining

Turning and remaking garments on the other side of the fabric used **Turning**
to be quite a normal practice in the days when materials were expensive and skilled dressmakers abundant. Now that new garments
include in their price a very high proportion of labour costs, it again
becomes economic to try this method of renovation. An old favourite
can be remade with up-to-date detail, and at the same time restored to
its original unworn texture and brightness of colour. Flannel or light
tweed coats are a good choice for turning. Not only will the material
have plenty of body, but their classic styles tend not to date.

THE FABRIC

Whether turning is feasible depends partly on the fabric. For instance,
napped or brushed materials, gaberdines or corded weaves will not
have the same appearance on the reverse side. Thin fabrics, when well
worn, may be so limp as to make turning hardly worth while. Prints
are obviously unsuitable. But many good woollen and worsted
materials, tweeds and hopsacks, and of course some silks, have a
reverse as well finished as the right side, and almost identical to it.

First of all, make sure that the material has not been affected by
wear. Hold it up to the light, to see whether there are any thin areas.
Look also at the front edges, collar, cuffs and armholes. Look inside
the lining; the reverse of the fabric will be as good as new both in
colour and texture, but interfacing may have been bonded to whole
panels, the surface of which might be affected by stripping it off. The
weave on the wrong side may be unattractive or show long 'floater'
threads.

If all is still well, then the first step is to unpick the whole garment
into its separate pieces, right down to the last dart. Press all seam
turnings out flat. Iron the garment pieces thoroughly, working along
the thread of the fabric to restore the correct shape to each panel.
Dry-cleaning or washing should be done at this stage, with the garment in pieces.

THE FRONT EDGES

The garment can usually be remade in its original size and style. But
if it shows wear down the front edges, the simplest and least conspicuous alteration would be to remake it in a slightly more fitted

style. By taking only 1.5 cm off each front edge, you could stitch a new seamline in firm, unworn fabric. Or a double-breasted style could be remade single-breasted.

Another possibility would be right-side facings; if you are shortening a long coat into a car-coat, for example, there should be plenty of matching fabric for new facings. Otherwise, consider using a contrasting material, or braid, or even leather (figure 5.1).

Figure 5.1

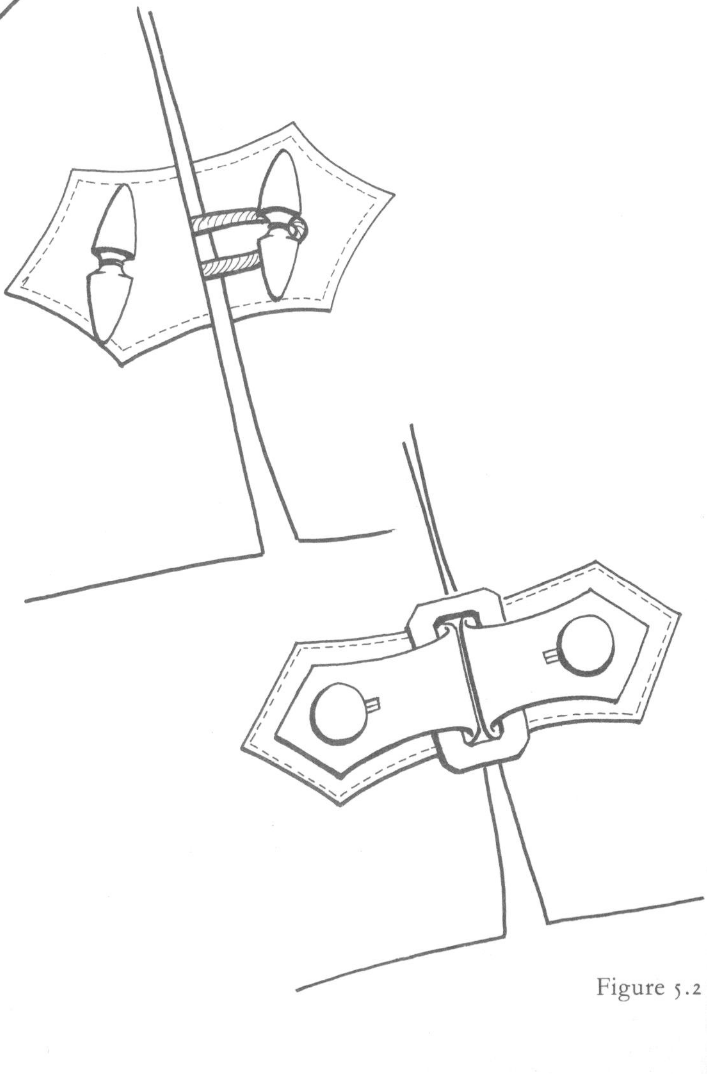

Figure 5.2

The most intractable problem is what to do about buttonholes. They will come on the wrong side of the body, and must first be sewn up. Then they can be covered either by right-side facings, or by strap fastenings. Instructions are given on page 48. A variation could be the tab-and-loop fastening, especially effective in leather on outdoor clothes (figure 5.2).

If the garment is easy-fitting, you could fasten it with an open-ended cardigan zip. In this case, the buttonholes would be trimmed off altogether (with an equal amount from the opposite side), and turnings of 1.5 cm made, as shown on page 51, before stitching in the zip. Make sure that the lower ends of the zipper-tapes are firmly finished off. Alternatively, where there will be facings, the tapes could be included into the seams (figure 5.3).

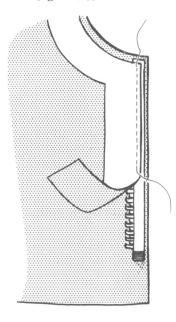

Figure 5.3

MAKING UP

Interfacing is important in building the shape of a garment, and you should use the same kind and weight as in the original. Iron-on woven interfacing with a fusible back is the type most likely to be found in ready-made garments; replace this with Moyceel or Staflex, or the new trellis-cut Vilene, all of which are available in the larger dress fabric departments. They are generally better than the plain non-woven interfacings, which can give rather too stiff an appearance.

Use the old pieces of interfacing as patterns, matching the direction of the thread. Iron on the interfacing through a damp cloth, or with a steam iron, pressing until it is firmly stuck down all over. Until the adhesive has become transparent (like cooked bacon-fat), the interfacing will not be properly bonded.

Darts and Seams   Make up the garment in the same order as you would a new one – darts and shaping first, then pockets, then the main seams.

The old fitting lines will probably still be visible; they will make accurate assembly easier, in fact, than if you were starting with new material. It is advisable to stitch a millimetre or so within these lines; such a small subtraction along the seams and darts will not affect the fit.

Pockets As there may have been pulling at the corners of pockets, you may need to make their openings a fraction longer. Recognize this problem early, and allow new fabric for a slightly longer slot, welt or pocket flap, as well as for a slightly wider pocket bag.

Collar If the collar pieces seem to have stretched along the neckline, they may be reinforced with tape, stitched into the seam as you attach the collar.

Lining You could not of course re-use the old lining. But take it apart in the same way as the rest of the garment, and use it as a pattern for the new lining.

Relining A lining is of great importance to the hang of a garment: do not be tempted to omit it. The lining of a dress is cut the same size as the dress itself. A skirt lining should be fractionally closer-fitting, to prevent seating. But the lining of a jacket should be looser, to avoid pulling up at the hem. A narrow pleat, for ease, should be laid down the centre-back, and the lining cut slightly longer at the sleeve and jacket hems. But if you use the old lining as your pattern, these extra measurements will already have been allowed for.

JACKET LINING

Although linings are usually set in by machine, a hand-felled lining is easier to manage; so this is the method shown here.

1 Stitch darts, side seams and shoulder seams by machine.
2 Press. Do not put in the sleeves yet.
3 Press a turning of 1.5 cm all round the neck, front facing and hem edges of the lining. With wrong sides together, pin the lining, along this fold, to the jacket. Fell in place (figure 5.4).

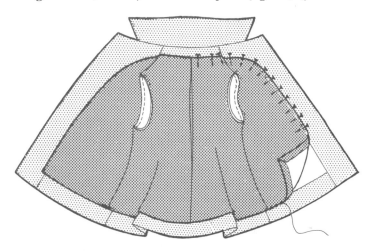

Figure 5.4

4 Machine stitch the sleeve seams of the lining.
5 Next, fell the wrist ends of the lining to the jacket wrist facing. This is easiest if you turn the sleeve inside out, and draw the lining (right side outside) over it, to match the wrist edges (figure 5.5).
7 Round the armhole, tack together the seam turnings of jacket and lining. At the top of the sleeve lining, turn in 1.5 cm, pin the fold over the armhole of the jacket lining, and fell. Distribute any fullness evenly around the sleevehead (figure 5.6).

Figure 5.5

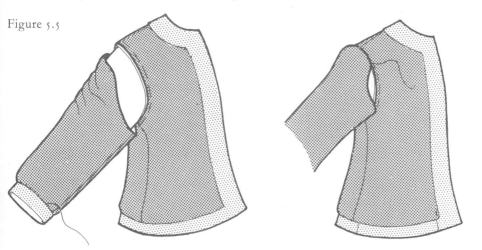

Figure 5.6

SKIRT LINING

Attach the lining after putting in the zip, and before setting on the waist finish.
1 Stitch the lining seams, leaving one open for the length of the zip.
2 Finish the hem of the lining by machine, making it 3–4 cm shorter than the skirt.
3 Place the skirt and lining with wrong sides facing, and tack together their waist edges. Set on the waistband or petersham, stitching through both skirt and lining. (See page 34.)
4 Fell the lining to the zipper-tapes, along each side of the opening (figure 5.7).

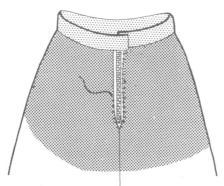

Figure 5.7

6 Remodelling

You cannot make a sow's ear into a silk purse, perhaps, but almost any garment, useless in its current form, may have possibilities for extensive remodelling. This chapter illustrates a number of typical styles, and suggests ways in which they might be remodelled either for yourself or for a child. You may not have a garment exactly the same as any shown here. No matter: once one understands the principles, it is not difficult to apply them to similar clothes.

Preparing the Material If you are completely remaking a garment, it should first be unpicked into its separate sections, and either dry-cleaned or washed in pieces. Make sure right at the start that old stitching marks, from darts or patch pockets, can be eradicated. Woollens will just need to be pressed under a damp cloth. Cottons and linens will lose any such marks in washing. There should be no problem with man-made fibres, or with any knitted fabrics. But silk and some rayons with a silky finish may not be so easy; if the marks will not come out, you must plan to avoid those areas in your layout.

Patterns and Layout Where no commercial pattern is needed, full instructions for making up are given here. But where a remodelled garment is totally different from the original, you would of course need to use a bought paper pattern, and follow its directions. The essential stage of fitting the pattern pieces onto the material of the old garment is shown in detail, because no pattern will help you there.

In ordinary dressmaking, starting from an uncut length of fabric, the pattern pieces are laid out with their grain-arrows exactly parallel to the selvedges. If this is not done, the garment will hang unevenly. Just the same applies to pattern layouts on an existing garment; but here there will be no guiding selvedges. First, therefore, look closely at the warp threads – the vertical threads when the garment is worn. Mark their direction, on each section of the garment, with a line of pins. Keep the pattern grain-arrows parallel to this line. If you have a pattern piece that has to be placed to a fold of the fabric, make sure that this fold, too, is on the straight grain.

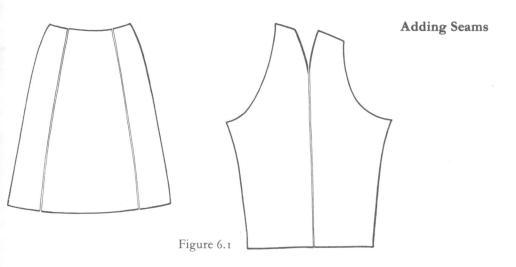

Adding Seams

Figure 6.1

If the old garment does not yield quite enough material for the planned one, do not be afraid of adding seams. One large piece may be impossible to fit on the area available; but two or three narrower pieces may quite easily be accommodated. You could, for instance, add two side-front seams to a skirt whose whole front was meant to be cut in one piece; or you could cut a Raglan sleeve in two halves, lengthways (figure 6.1). To add a seam, simply cut the pattern piece from end to end, and allow 1.5 cm for a turning along each cut edge.

Have you a good dress, unwearable only because of an old-fashioned or unflattering collar? With a new, lower-cut neckline and no sleeves, it could be brought up to date as a pinafore dress, to wear over shirts (see illustration 2 on page 33). This is a simple alteration which should present no difficulties (figure 6.2).

Dress into Pinafore Dress

Figure 6.2

1 Remove the collar and neckline facings.
2 Try on the dress. Mark with pins the new lines for neck and armholes. The neckline can be cut to any shape you wish; but if you retain the same height at the back of the neck you will not have to reset the back zip. Keep the line close to the neck at the sides: it will sit better. If you plan to cut the armholes deeper, you may need to take in the bodice side seams a little, to give a good fit (figure 6.3).
3 Cut away the surplus material at neck and shoulder, leaving 1.5 cm beyond the pins, for seam turnings.

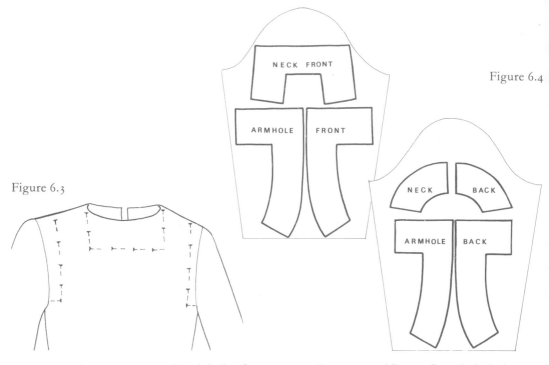

Figure 6.4

Figure 6.3

4 Unpick the sleeve seams. Cut new neckline and armhole facings, as shown on page 113, from the sleeves. The facings may be pieced if necessary (figure 6.4).
5 Stitch the seams of the facings, and press open. Stitch the facings to the dress, right sides together. Clip the turnings at corners and

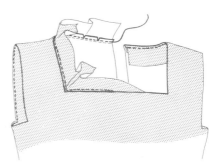

Figure 6.5

curves. Edge-stitch the facings and turnings together, to prevent the neckline from rolling over (figure 6.5).

6 Turn the facings to the inside of the pinafore dress, and press. Catch down their edges at the shoulder and underarm seams, to hold them in place.

Suit into Dress

Those useful knitted suits – of polyester or acrylic jersey – can become out-of-date before their fabric shows any signs of wear. The skirt may be the wrong length, or the proportions of the jacket may now be dowdy. But it may well be worth while remaking the suit into a shirt-waister dress. The skirt would gain at least 3 cm extra length by being released from its waistband, and could be let down further at the hem. The useful, between-seasons dress shown here (figure 6.6) was made from a Crimplene suit. The alteration is very simple.

Figure 6.6

1 Put on and fasten the jacket. Using tailor's chalk, mark in the exact waist level. If you are not sure, tie a piece of string round your waist, and mark along the string.

2 Trim off the lower edge of the jacket, leaving 5 cm (a good safety margin) below the marked waistline.

3 Pin two front and two back waist darts. Their width will depend on your figure and on the cut of the jacket, but you would expect each front dart to be at least 1.5 cm at its widest, from fold to stitching; and each back dart about 1 cm. The object is to give the jacket reasonable fit at and just above the waistline. Do not over-fit – the waist should be 6 cm wider than your own waist measurement. Back darts should be about 15 cm long, and front darts should taper to nothing 3 cm below the point of the bust (figure 6.7). If there are darts in the skirt, arrange the bodice darts to correspond to them.

Figure 6.7

4 On the wrong side of the bodice, mark with tailor's chalk along both sides of each dart. Unpin the darts, re-pin them along the chalked lines (with the darts now on the inside of the garment), and stitch. Press the darts towards the centre-back and centre-front. On thick fabrics, slash the darts along the fold, and press their edges open (figure 6.8).

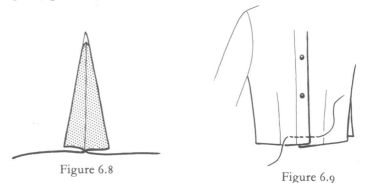

Figure 6.8

Figure 6.9

5 Button together the bodice fronts. 1 cm below the waistline, stitch the right and left sides together, to hold them in the buttoned position (figure 6.9).
6 Unpick the left underarm seam for 10 cm above the waistline, for the zip opening.
7 Take off the waistband of the skirt, and take out the zip. Leave the left side seam of the skirt open for 20 cm below the waist. Keep any skirt lining in place, if it is fit to be used again.

8 Check that the skirt waistline has the same measurement as the bodice; alter the darts if necessary.

9 Put the bodice inside the skirt, with right sides together, matching their waistlines. Tack them together round the waistline, starting and finishing at the left-side opening. (Remember that you may still have some extra length on the bodice, below the marked waistline.) Try on, and pin together the side opening, to make sure of the fit and level of the waistline. Machine. (Figure 6.10.)

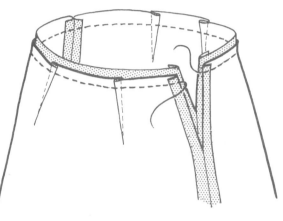

Figure 6.10

10 Insert a 30 cm zip into the left underarm seam, following the instructions on page 50.

11 If the sleeves now look too heavy for the style of the dress, they could be shortened to below or just above the elbow. A neat sleeve finish would be a facing top-stitched to the right side of the sleeve, to match the bands down the bodice. Cut from the surplus jacket fabric strips long enough to go round the sleeve, plus 3 cm; and as wide as the front bands, plus 3 cm. Seam the narrow ends together, with 1.5 cm turnings. Press the seam open.

With the *right* side of the band to the *wrong* side of the sleeve, (figure 6.11), stitch the seam all round the sleeve (A). Turn the band to the right side of the sleeve, and press (B). Fold in 1.5 cm along the free edge, and top-stitch the band close to the fold (C).

12 Finish the dress with a bought belt, or one made from fabric left over from the jacket. (See page 52.)

Figure 6.11

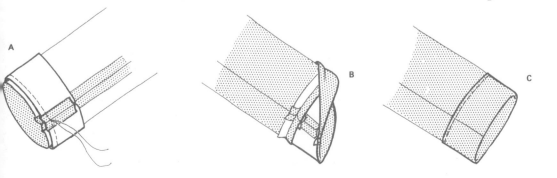

Knitted Suit into Over-sweater Do not despise the potential of your outsize aunt's cast-offs. Those generously-cut double jersey suits may be sadly out of date, yet provide plenty of good material in reasonably large pieces. The jacket and skirt together would make into a really large, loose over-sweater, to wear with trousers. The one shown in figure 6.12 and illustration 3 (see page 39) was made in a firm jersey with a pronounced horizontal rib.

Figure 6.12

THE PATTERN

The pattern shown here is suitable for knits, not for woven fabrics. A bought pattern will not be needed; just draw the pattern pieces on newspaper (figure 6.13). (All measurements are in centimetres.)

As in any remake, you may have to adjust the exact measurements to the fabric available. In this case, the critical measurements are the length and width of the jacket back. If you have ample material here, you can cut the back pattern wider below the armholes, or longer; then make the same additions to the front, below the yoke.

Figure 6.13

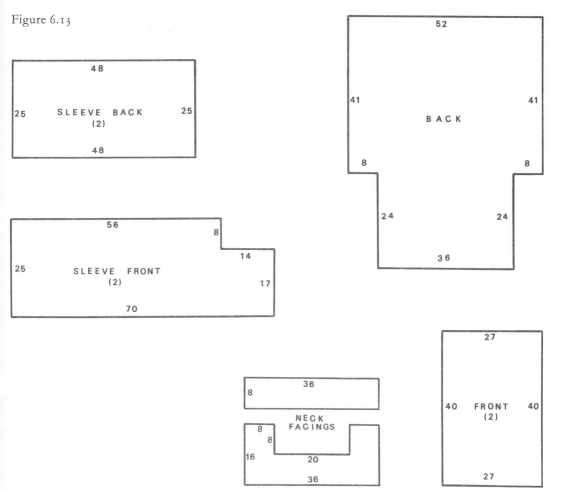

1 Cut out the paper pattern.
2 Unpick the skirt into its separate pieces.
3 Take out the sleeves, and unpick their underarm seams.
4 Take out the jacket back complete, leaving intact any side-back or
   centre-back seams. Unpick shoulder and waist darts, and press out
   their creases.
5 Lay the pattern out as in figure 6.14:
      The neck facings on one front of the jacket. (A)
      The back on the jacket back. (B)
      The sleeve backs on two skirt panels. (C)
      The sleeve fronts on the other two skirt panels. (D)
      The fronts on the sleeves. (E)

TO MAKE UP
Take 1 cm seam turnings throughout.
1 Stitch the sleeve backs to the bodice back, in an angled seam. Work
   with the bodice uppermost. When you come to the corner, leave
   the machine needle down, raise the presser foot, and clip the bodice

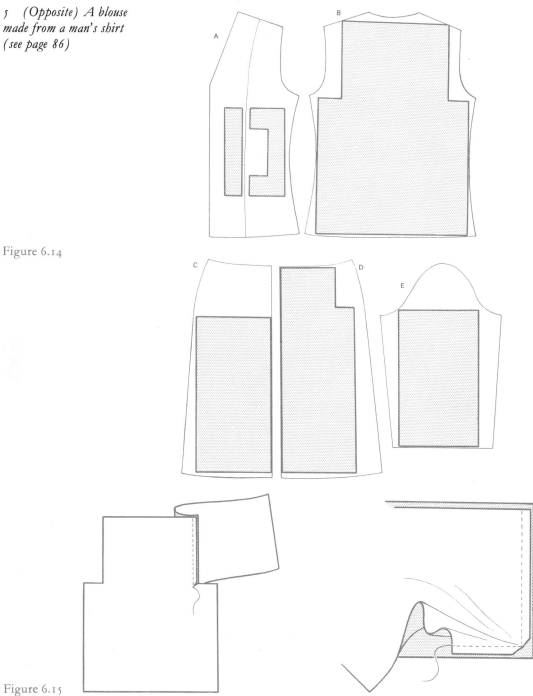

5 (Opposite) A blouse made from a man's shirt (see page 86)

Figure 6.14

Figure 6.15

seam allowance almost to the stitching. This will allow you to pull the bodice right round to match its edge with that of the sleeve, beyond the corner. Lower the presser foot, and stitch the rest of the seam (figure 6.15).

2 Stitch the shoulder seams, matching the back and front sleeves at their outer ends. The fronts will overlap at the centre; fold in these edges for the centre buttoning, and tack them together (figure 6.16).

Figure 6.16

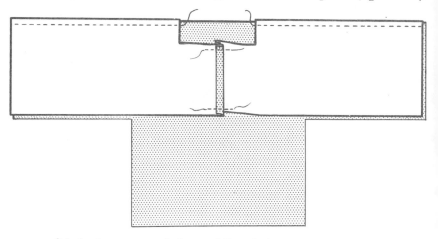

3 Stitch the seams of the neckline facings, and press them open (figure 6.17).

Figure 6.17

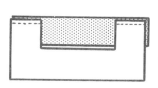 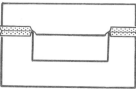

4 Stitch the facings to the neckline, right sides together. Clip the inner corners, turn the facings to the inside, and press (figure 6.18).

Figure 6.18

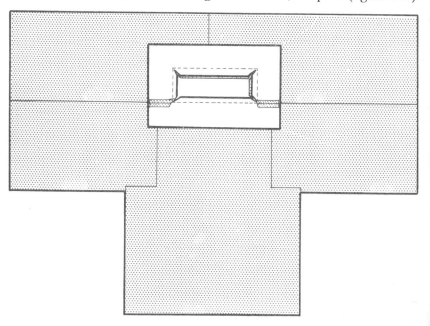

5 Catch down the free edge of the facing to the shoulder seams. Sew two buttons on the right front, stitching through all the thicknesses, including the facing. (These buttons are purely decorative; you need not work buttonholes.)

6 Stitch together the two fronts, down one long edge. Stitch the fronts to the sleeve fronts, matching at the centre (figure 6.19).

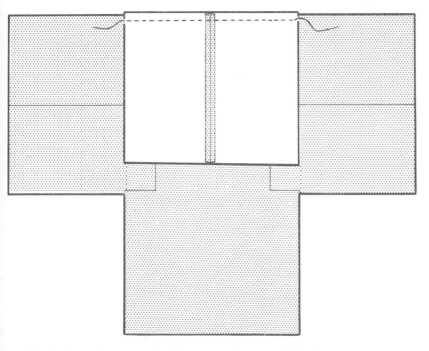

Figure 6.19

7 Stitch the underarm and side seams all as one. Clip the seam turnings at the underarm corner (figure 6.20).

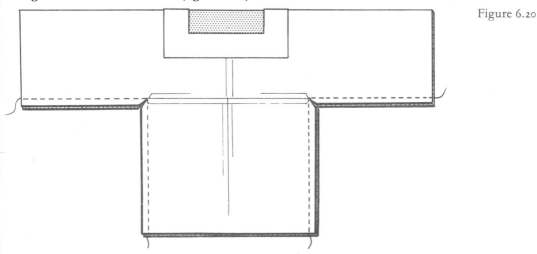

Figure 6.20

8 Turn up 5 cm hems on the sleeves and at the lower edge of the sweater. Catch-stitch in place, as shown on page 19.

Coat into Gored Skirt

Figure 6.21

A gored skirt can very easily be made from a waisted and flared coat. The skirt shown in illustration 4 (page 49) and figure 6.21 is eight-gored, made from a wool coating that would normally be considered too heavy for a skirt – but with such body, it hangs beautifully. This is an excellent use for a coat that is too short: the skirt patterns can be placed a little higher on the coat, to give extra length. There should be plenty of fabric, but you will need to plan the number of gores according to the panels of the coat.

If the coat has centre-back, side-back and side-front seams as in figure 6.22, you would be able to cut an eight-gored skirt from the eight panels. But if the right-front panel has buttonholes *below* the waistline, some of its width may be unusable. In this case, it could be better to make a seven-gored skirt, using the left-front panel for the centre-front, flanked by the old side-front panels. At any rate, in a double-breasted style, there should still be enough 'girth'.

If there is no centre-back seam then use the whole back panel for the *centre-front* of the skirt. Put the two front panels at the *back*; with the zip between them. With the four side-pieces, you would then have a seven-gored skirt, with a front panel wider than the others (figure 6.23).

If the coat is close-fitting, some of the existing seams could even be used in the skirt. No pattern would be needed, and the skirt could be fitted on the figure. First, tack up the new centre-front seam; try on; and then make any adjustments at the side-seams.

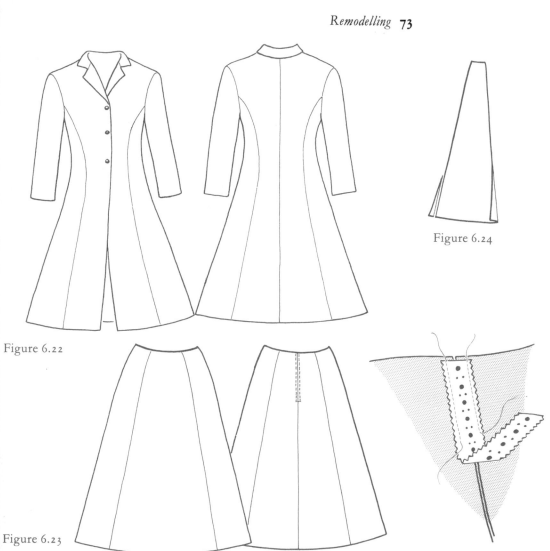

Figure 6.24

Figure 6.22

Figure 6.23

Figure 6.25

Width at the hem   A coat should give plenty of fabric at waist and hip level; but with a very flared skirt, you may have difficulty in accommodating the width at the hem. If there is not quite enough fabric here, you could try one of two expedients. One way is to make the flare a little less pronounced, trimming off or folding back 2–3 cm from each edge of the pattern (figure 6.24).

Alternatively, dispense with the seam allowances and make strap seams instead, perhaps using bands of suède pinked along their edges and punched with holes. For this type of seam, lay the edges of the two skirt panels together (not overlapping); lay the strap over the seamline, and machine close to each edge of the strap (figure 6.25). As you cannot tack or pin through suède, hold it temporarily in place on the fabric with a little Copydex; this will harm neither the suède nor the fabric, and will disappear in dry-cleaning. Interesting details of style, such as this, can often be suggested by sheer necessity – and none the worse for that.

When you have stitched the seams, set in the zip, as shown on page 50. Finish the waistline with a petersham ribbon, as shown on page 34. Turn up the hem and catch-stitch in place – see page 19.

Trousers into Skirt If this operation is possible at all, it will not be difficult. The limiting factor is the width round the leg. Narrow, closely-fitting trousers (because their side seams will be shaped inwards on the thigh), will not yield enough fabric for even the slimmest of skirts. But French-cut or bell-bottomed trousers are a different matter: with careful placing of the pattern, a straight or very slightly flared four-panel skirt, as shown in figure 6.26, can usually be cut from the four trouser pieces.

Figure 6.26

But remember that trouser fabric will not usually have enough body, even though firmly-woven, to hang well as an unlined skirt. A lining is well worth the small extra time and expense involved. Cut it from the same pattern as the skirt, just shortening it by 5 cm at the hem. Consider pockets at this stage (page 53); there will be plenty of fabric for them.

1 First, unpick all the trouser seams. Be especially careful not to cut any threads of fabric along the leg seams – this is where you will need the greatest width.
2 Wash and press the four pieces.
3 The layout of your pattern will depend on the cut of the trousers. It is unlikely that the obvious one – with waistlines matching – will give enough room for the pattern.

4 Pair up the trouser pieces, with right sides together. Pin your pattern to the double thickness, keeping it true to the straight grain of the fabric. Cut the fronts of the skirt from the trouser fronts, the backs from the backs.

5 Stitch the side seams of the skirt, and set in the zip (page 50).

6 Make up the lining. Tack it to the waistline of the skirt, with wrong sides together. Fell the opening edges to the zipper tapes.

7 Finish the waist with a petersham ribbon, attached as shown on page 34.

8 Turn up and finish the hem by catch-stitching (see page 19). The lining hem should be machined.

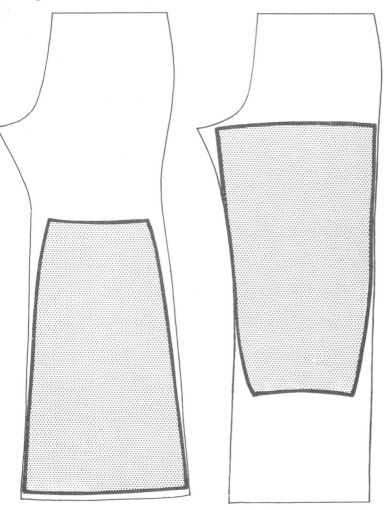

Figure 6.27

On trousers that are very wide at the hem, the pattern may be best placed with its hem at that level too, as in the left-hand sketch in figure 6.27. But if the trouser crutch is cut wide, you may do better to reverse the pattern, getting extra hem width at this point, as in the right-hand sketch.

Trousers into Children's Clothes The quality of trouser fabric, and the quantity available, both lend themselves well to children's clothes. A girl's skirt could easily be cut from trousers not wide enough to make an adult's, following the instructions above. But you could also consider making boys' or girls' trousers, or dungarees. The pedal-pushers shown in illustration 9, page 105, could have been made from an adult's trousers (figure 6.28).

Figure 6.28

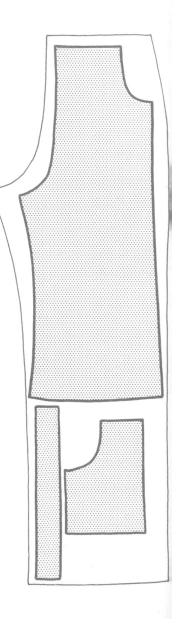

Dress into Shirt-Jacket

Figure 6.29

It would be possible to turn a tired dress of unfashionable length into an unlined jacket. The dress shown in figure 6.29 was in a lightweight, striped flannel, with the stripes used attractively as cross-banding down the front. But it fitted too tightly round the hips and had seated badly; it was too short; and it tended to gape where the fly-fastening buttoned through to an inside petersham ribbon. In fact, it was unwearable in that state. But it remodelled very successfully into a light summer jacket.

1 Cut off the skirt 5 cm below the end of the front opening. (This 5 cm will form the hem.)
2 Unpick the seam across the bottom end of the opening, and the short section of seam below it. Take out the petersham buttonhole-strip.
3 If the fabric is limp, give it extra body just along the 5 cm hem turning, by ironing on a strip of fusible woven interfacing, such as Moyceel or Staflex.
4 Unpick the inside edge of the facing band at its lower end, and open it out. (A—B in figure 6.30.)
5 Turn the facing inside out, along the fold, and machine-stitch close to its lower edge, through both thicknesses. (B—A in figure 6.31.)

Figure 6.30

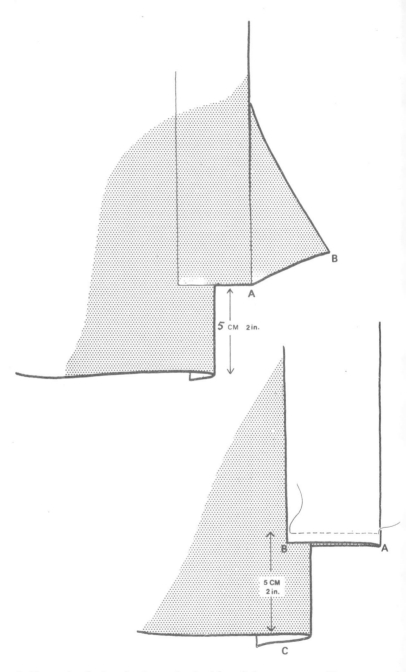

Figure 6.31

6 Turn the facing back to the inside of the garment. Turn up and press the hem (c), bringing it level with the end of the band (A–B in figure 6.32). Finish the hem by catch-stitching.

7 To secure the free edge of the facing, top-stitch by machine, with the right side of the garment uppermost, close to the inner edge of the front band. This stitching will sink invisibly into the seam (figure 6.33).

Figure 6.32

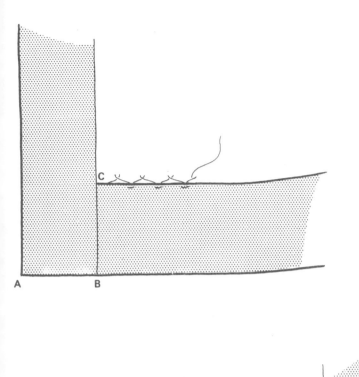

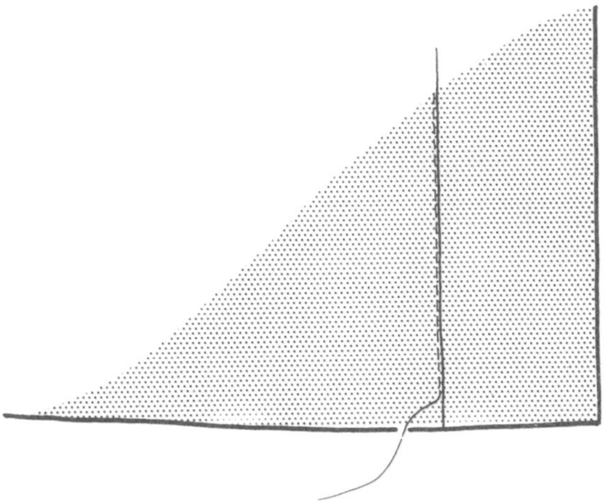

Figure 6.33

8 Mark the buttonhole placings down the right-hand band. The top
   one would be marked at whatever level is fashionable; one buttonhole should be placed at the waistline, unless there is to be a belt.
   In this case, because the bands were horizontally striped, the
   buttonholes were also set horizontally. If there were no stripes,
   however, the buttonholes could be set vertically, as on a shirt – this
   would be appropriate for thin fabrics.
9 Make the buttonholes by machine as shown on page 47.
10 Mark the position for each button with a pin, through its buttonhole, and sew on.
11 The discarded skirt would provide enough fabric to make a belt, if
   one were needed, or patch pockets.

**Two into One Will Go
– Bride's Mother's
Outfit into Dress**

Figure 6.34

Nothing dates itself more firmly than the silky dress-and-coat ensemble designed for a formal occasion. The style could be too straight and unsympathetic for the more fluid feeling of clothes today. Yet the garments will probably have had little wear and the material is likely to be interesting. The very quantity of fabric available in the two garments would make remodelling an excellent proposition.

You could design a softer style, with shirring and gathers, provided that the material is supple enough to handle in this way. The style shown in figure 6.34 was taken straight from a 1939 fashion magazine. After almost forty years we have come round so nearly to the feeling of that time, that neither the proportions nor any detail of the original style needed altering; even the shoulder buttons look right. The centre panel gives a long, slimming line. This would be a fairly lengthy but not complicated transformation.

1 First, try on the dress. Mark with pins the proposed outline for the centre-front panel. Shape it slightly in at the waist, and then wider towards the hem. Mark also with pins the levels for the yoke and the waistline shirring (figure 6.35).

2 Fold the dress in half down the centre-front. Place the fold to the right-hand edge of a sheet of newspaper. Transfer the pin-markings for the front panel to the newspaper, as shown on page 106. Also mark in the neck and hem edges. Do not at this stage allow for any turnings. You will now have a half-pattern for the centre-front panel; cut this from the *coat*, folded in half down the centre-back. Lay the newspaper pattern to the fold and cut out, allowing 1.5 cm for turnings at neck and side edges, and at the hem a turning of the same depth as on the dress (figure 6.36).

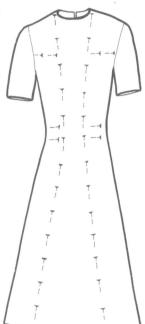

Figure 6.35

Figure 6.36

Figure 6.37

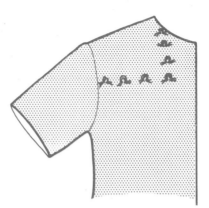

3 With the dress still folded down the centre-front, tailor-tack along the pin-marking for the lower edge of the yoke, and for the side of the yoke. (This makes certain that both sides will be identical.) (Figure 6.37.)

4 Cut the tailor's tacks and open out the dress. Now begin to take it to pieces. Unpick the armhole seams and take out the sleeves. Unpick the back and front neckline facings; these could be used again, or you could cut new ones from the dress sleeves. Unpick and press out any front shaping darts.

Figure 6.38

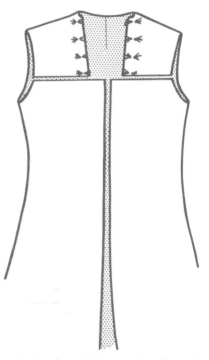

6 (Opposite) A blouse made from a dress that had become too short (see page 89)

5 Cut right across the bodice, following the line of tailor's tacks. Cut away the surplus fabric *between* the two yokes, but leave 1.5 cm at each side for seam turnings. Slash the dress exactly down the centre-front, from yoke level to hem (figure 6.38).

6 Gather each side of the dress to fit its yoke. Stitch the yoke to the gathered edge, making the narrowest seam possible (figure 6.39).

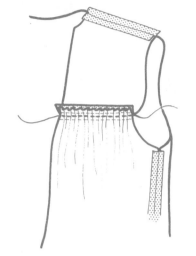

Figure 6.39

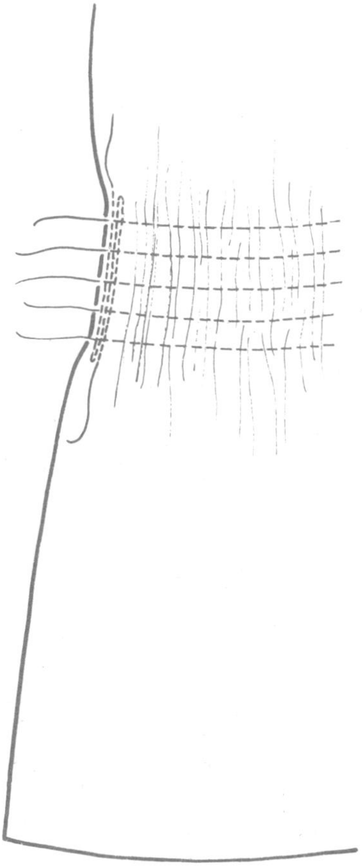

Figure 6.40

7 Now work the waistline shirring. Use elastic thread, hand-wound on the machine bobbin. Do not change the needle-thread. Set the longest possible stitch. Working from the right side, begin machining at the very edge of one side-front. Stitch right round the side and back of the dress, to the front again. The rows of shirring should be not more than 1 cm apart; to space them evenly, stitch with the edge of the presser-foot level with the previous row of shirring. Secure the ends of the shirring threads by machining several times across them, within the seam allowance (figure 6.40).
8 Stitch the new centre panel to the two side panels, from hem edge up to the shoulder, crossing the shirring on the way. Finish the hemline.

9 Stitch the front and back neck facings together at the shoulder
   seams. With facings and dress right-sides-together, stitch all round
   the neckline. Clip the seam turnings, and edge-stitch the facings to
   the turnings, as shown on page 63, to stop the neckline edge from
   rolling over. Turn the facings to the inside, and press.
10 Cut new sleeves and sleeve-bands from the sleeves of the coat – or
   from its sides or fronts. Use any full sleeve pattern, shortened if
   necessary. The sleeve-bands should be cut 10 cm deep (to give a
   finished depth of about 3.5 cm), and long enough for a close fit at
   the upper forearm, allowing 3 cm for turnings.
11 Stitch the underarm seam of each sleeve, gather the lower edge, and
   set on the sleeve-band (figures 6.41 and 6.42).

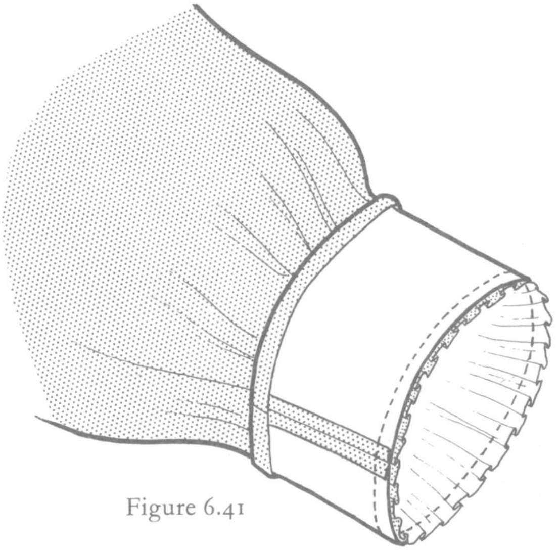

Figure 6.41

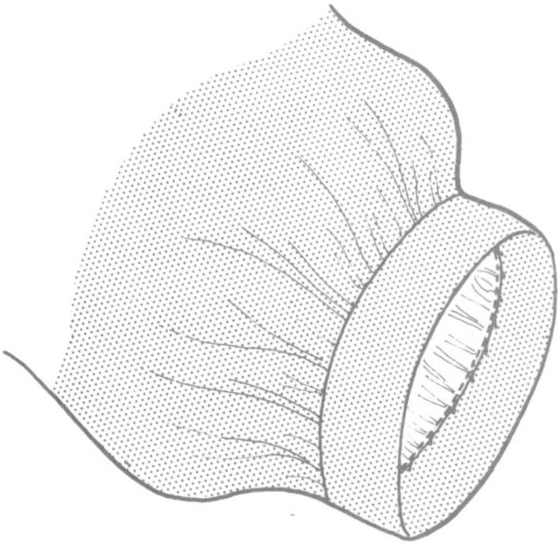

Figure 6.42

12 Check the fit of the armhole. As the yoke seam will have taken a
   centimetre or so out of the front edge of the armhole, you could cut
   this lower under the arm by not more than 5 mm; but this should
   not be necessary. Pin and tack the sleeves into their armholes,
   following the instructions on page 44, and gathering the head of
   the sleeve to fit. Stitch round the armhole seam, and neaten the
   turnings with zigzag machining.
13 Sew four or five small bobble buttons along each shoulder seam.

**Man's Shirt into
Blouse**

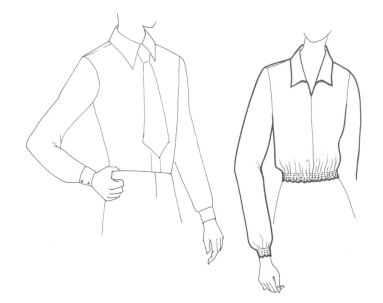

Figure 6.43

When the collar of a shirt wears through, one can of course turn it. But even when collar and cuffs are both frayed, the body of the shirt may still be in good condition. Every family must have such a relic. Here (figure 6.43) is a suggestion for making it into a shirred blouse, to be worn by itself or over a high-necked sweater. The blouse could have a centre-front seam, as shown above; or else an open-ended zip, as in illustration 5 (see page 69).

1 Unpick the collar from the shirt, leaving the shirt seam turnings intact. Unpick the stitching down the left front, and cut off the edge level with the buttonholes. Unpick the stitching down the right front and take off the buttons. Unpick the shirt hem. Unpick the cuffs from the sleeves, leaving the sleeve openings intact. Press out all creases.

2 Cut off the bottom 15 cm of the shirt. This will be used for the new collar.

3 Turn up a 6 cm hem round the lower edge of the shirt, fold in 1 cm, and tack.

4 Check the sleeve length. Can you turn up a 6 cm hem at the wrist, without needing a false hem? If not, cut false hems 7 cm deep from discarded front sections of the shirt. Apply them as shown on page 22. Turn up and tack as for the waistline edge.

5 Now work the shirring. Wind the bobbin of the machine, by hand, with shirring elastic. Set the longest stitch. Work four evenly-spaced rows of shirring, through the tacked hems of bodice and sleeves. Begin and end at the very edges of the fabric. Secure the ends of the shirring elastic by stitching across them several times, within the seam allowance. (See figure on page 84.)

6 At the wrists, stitch up the sleeve openings, taking into the seam the ends of the shirring (figure 6.44).

Figure 6.44

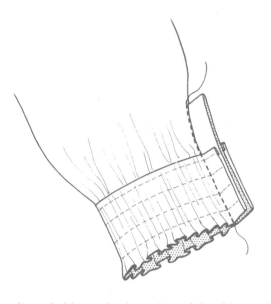

7 From the discarded lower back section of the shirt, make the new
collar. Cut it as long as possible, from side-seam to side-seam, and
use the full 15 cm depth. Cut a strip of white lawn for interfacing,
7.5 cm deep. Fold the collar right sides together, lay the interfacing
on top, and stitch the seam at each end. Trim, turn and press
(figure 6.45).

Figure 6.45

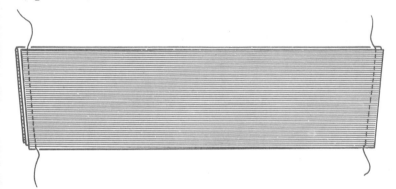

8 Now you are ready to try on the shirt, and mark the new neckline.
Tack together the two front edges. Pin on the collar, to help you
judge how deep the v should be. Mark the new neckline with pins.
Keep its shaping close to the neck at the sides, to meet the old
collar seamline at the shoulders (figure 6.46).
9 Stitch the centre-front seam, from hem level, through the shirring,
up to the neckline.
10 Trim away the surplus fabric at the neck, leaving 1.5 cm for seam
turnings beyond the pinned edge. Make patterns for the back and
front neck facings, as shown on page 113. Cut the facings from
scraps of white lawn; seam them together at the shoulders and centre
front; and press open the seams.

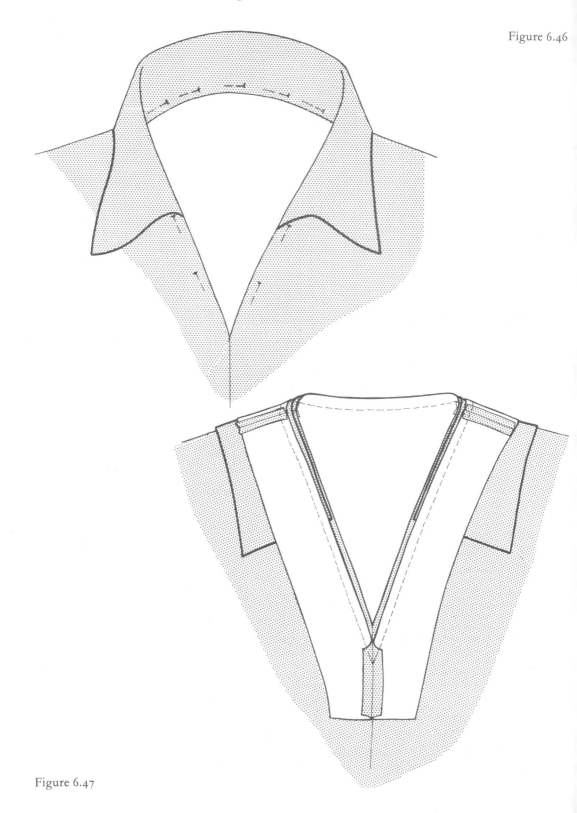

Figure 6.46

Figure 6.47

11 Now lay the collar in place round the neckline, right side up. Lay the facings on top, wrong side up, and tack. Machine all round the neck as one seam, pivoting at the point of the v (figure 6.47).
12 Clip the seam turnings at corners and curves, and edge-stitch as shown on page 62, to stop the neckline from rolling over.

Dress into Blouse

The blouse in illustration 6 (page 83) was made from a dress that was too short to wear. The centre-front seam was simply unpicked, and the zip set in from the waistline upwards. The flip-tie belt was made from strips of fabric cut from the skirt. It was set on in the same way as a band is set on a gathered sleeve; see page 85.

Revamping a Suit

A suit with a generally discouraged air could be drastically re-cut to eliminate any out-dated features such as the shape of the collar, the level of the buttons or the fit of the jacket. A light-weight suit could be given new fashion life by turning it into a bolero outfit, as shown in figure 6.48. First, unpick and take off the jacket collar and facings. Unpick waistline darts, and press. Now take a long, critical look at what you have left.

1 Using pins to mark the lines, experiment with new shapes to the neck and front edges. Try marking the front edges well apart from each other, away from buttonholes or worn edges. Mark also a new, shorter length to the jacket; this may look well if it is 5–8 cm above the true waistline. Pin a new length to the sleeves. Consider whether a turned-back cuff would add interest.
2 When you are satisfied, place left and right sides of the jacket together, matching them exactly. Mark the new neckline and front edges with tailor's tacks through both thicknesses (as shown on page 16). Cut the tacks, and open out the jacket.
3 Cut off the surplus fabric, but leave 1.5 cm turnings at neck and front edges, and 4–5 cm for the hem turning. Do not cut away the lining yet.
4 Cut patterns for the new front and neckline facings – you may be able to use the two strips discarded from the button side of the jacket.
5 Stitch the back-neck facing to the front facings. With right sides together, stitch the facings to the neckline and front edges. Clip the turnings along curves, turn the facings to the inside, and press.
6 Turn up the hem, and press. Catch-stitch in place, as shown on page 19.
7 Make and attach any patch pockets. (See page 53.) You may be able to make these from the old ones. Pockets above the waistline should be small – experiment with cut paper shapes and sizes until you are satisfied.
8 Next, turn to the sleeves. On a straight-cut sleeve, just make a deep hem, finished with catch-stitching; and turn it up to form the cuff. (Below the finished sleeve-length, allow twice the depth of the cuff plus 4 cm.)

Figure 6.48

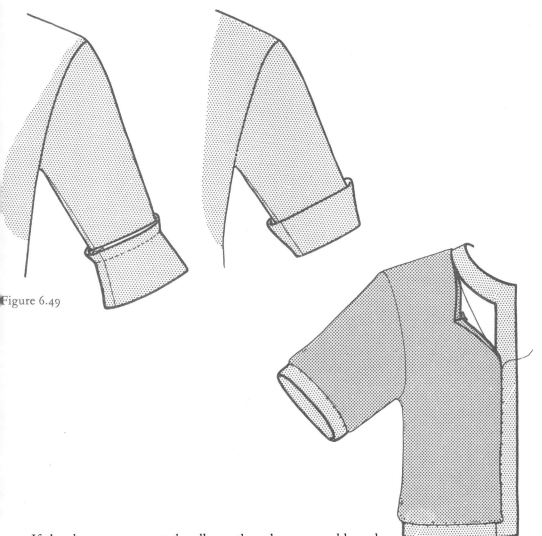

Figure 6.49

Figure 6.50

If the sleeve narrows at the elbow, though, you would need a separate cuff, made from the surplus fabric. Cut it twice the depth you want the finished cuff to be, plus 3 cm for turnings (figure 6.49).

9 Now trim the lining to size. Let it overlap, by 3 cm, the neck and front facings. Fold in 1.5 cm along the lining edge here, and fell in place over the facings.

Along the lower edge, cut the lining to the length of the *finished* jacket hem; fold under 1.5 cm along the edge of the lining and fell this fold 3 cm above the jacket edge. This will give a little extra length, to prevent pulling at the hem. Never cut a lining exactly the same length as the jacket – there should always be a little extra ease.

At the sleeves, trim off the lining level with the cuff. Fold under 1.5 cm, and fell inside the sleeve (figure 6.50).

10 An eight-button trim would pull the design together. For other ways of treating front edges, see pages 45–7.

Ties Men's ties are expensive to make from bought material, as they are cut on the bias and take up at least 50 cm of fabric. A tie without any seams would actually need a full square metre, most of it wasted. In factory production, the patterns are laid side by side, diagonally across the fabric – an economical layout when a number of ties are to be cut. But remnants of material you already have may be enough for a tie. The one shown in illustration 7 (page 95) was made from pieces left over from a moiré skirt.

Any fabric with plenty of body will make a good tie. You could use a firm silk or acetate, a fine wool or even thin tweed. The main consideration is that the material should have substance, otherwise it may pull out of shape at the knot.

As well as the tie fabric, you will need lining and interfacing. The lining should be a thin silk, rayon or Tricel; quite small pieces will do, seamed together. Special tie interfacing – a very springy fabric – can be found in good dress fabric departments. You will need 50 cm. It is possible to make a tie without interfacing, but then the knot will be smaller and the tie may stretch. On the other hand, it could be washable.

THE PATTERN

Take two sheets of newspaper – one the size of national daily papers (83 × 61 cm) and the other the size of local or evening papers (61 × 44 cm). It just happens that these sizes will give exactly the right length for a tie, so the pattern can be measured out easily and cut accurately. See figure 6.51.

1 Fold each sheet as shown, bringing down the top left-hand corner to the lower edge (A). Crease from the lower left-hand corner (B) to the upper edge (C), to give a true diagonal.

2 On the larger sheet, measure and mark 19 cm from the corner along the lower edge (B–D). At the top, mark 7 cm from the crease towards the right (C–E).

3 Rule a line D–E.

4 Cut through both thicknesses of newspaper, from D to E.

5 On the smaller sheet, measure and mark 8 cm from the corner along the lower edge (B–F). At the top, mark 7 cm from the crease towards the right (C–G). Join F–G.

6 Cut out through both thicknesses, from F to G.

7 Unfold both pattern pieces. Overlap their diagonal ends 1 cm, and stick together (figure 6.52).

This pattern will give a tie long enough for a Windsor knot, and with a finished width of 14 cm across the end. For a wider or narrower tie, simply move point D on the pattern to right or left.

CUTTING OUT

The tie must be cut on the true cross of the fabric, or it will wrinkle and pull in wear. If you have no selvedge to guide you, put a row of pins down the warp thread of the fabric, and be sure that one square

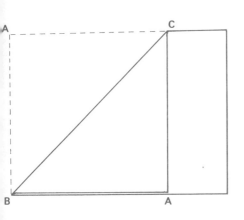

Figure 6.51

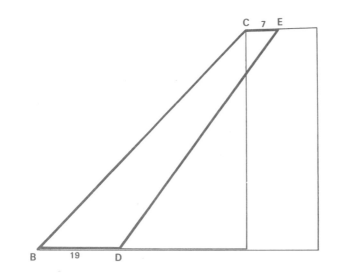

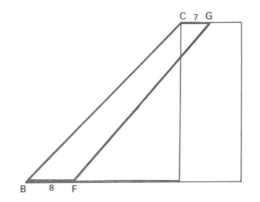

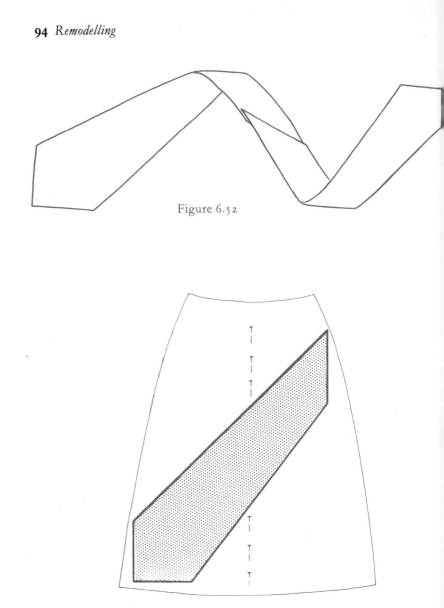

Figure 6.52

Figure 6.53

end of the pattern lies parallel to the pins (figure 6.53). Cut as long a piece as possible, at least 70 cm, for the wide end of the tie; beyond that, you will need one seam, possibly two, to get the length. For each seam, add 2 cm for seam turnings. The seams must be stitched along the straight grain of the fabric, parallel to the join in the pattern. Be sure to allow for this when cutting out the pieces. Cut the tie and lining to the same pattern.

For the interfacing, fold the pattern edges-to-middle, and overlap the edges a bare 2 cm. Fold up 20 cm at the wide end and 12 cm at the narrow end of the pattern. (Interfacing is not needed at the ends of the

7 (Opposite) A tie made from a moiré skirt (see page 92)

tie.) Cut from the altered pattern, on the bias of the interfacing (figure 6.54).

Figure 6.54

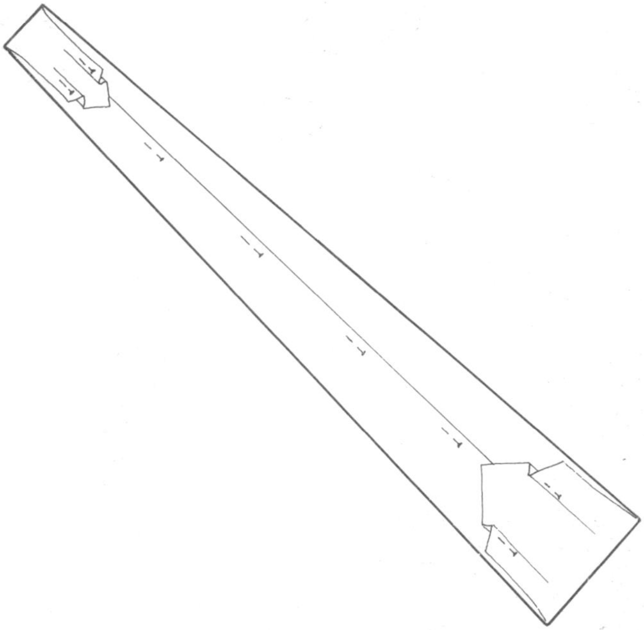

MAKING UP

1 Stitch the seams of the tie and lining, so that each is in one piece. Press the seams open.

2 Now finish both ends of the tie. Match the square ends to their linings, right sides together, and machine 1 cm from the edges, beginning and ending 7 or 8 cm above the corners. Clip the seam allowance at the ends of the machining (figure 6.55).

3 Trim the corners, turn and press.

4 With the tie still right-side-out, fold it in half lengthways – with the right side of the lining outside. The seamline for the one long seam is 1 cm in from the edges. Match this to the centre-line of the tie interfacing (a pencilled line will help) and pin together. Be very precise here; unless you are accurate, the tie will go wavy (figure 6.56).

5 Either machine this seam, through all five thicknesses; or, better, sew it by hand with loose running stitches. Begin and end just above the finished ends of the tie.

6 Turn the tie right-side-out by putting a safety-pin in its thin end, and threading through.

7 Press carefully, with the seam down the centre. To avoid transferring the mark of the seam to the right side of the tie, cut a piece of stiff cardboard to the shape of the wide end, and slip this inside the tie before pressing.

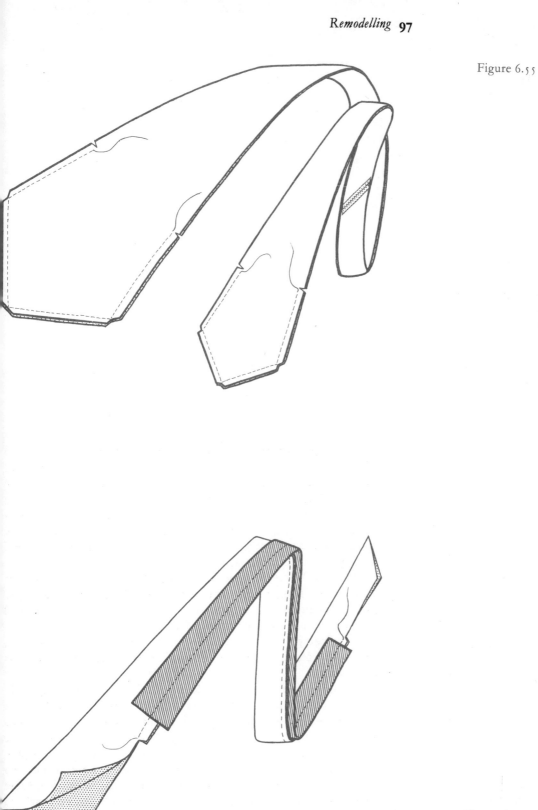

Figure 6.55

Figure 6.56

**Father's Gaberdine
Raincoat into Anorak**

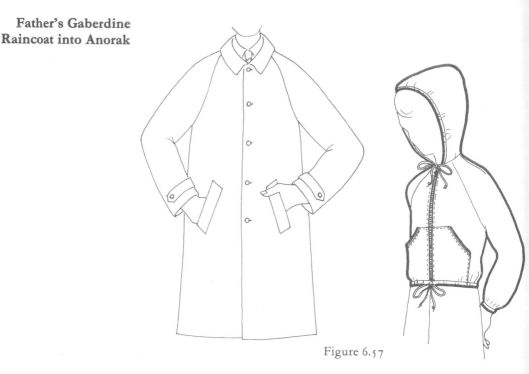

Figure 6.57

Every household must surely have, in the garage or potting shed, an old gaberdine raincoat – used only for the dirtiest jobs, and surviving simply because it would disgrace a jumble sale. Perhaps it will be one of those indestructible Burberrys: the anorak shown in figure 6.57 and illustration 8 (see page 99) was made from exactly that – a Burberry that had hung on the back of the cellar door for twenty-five years, covered with paint stains, dejected, but still sound.

Its appalling state is stressed simply because most people have some such skeleton. Yet these raincoats, if originally good, have an almost indefinite life. Their fabric is of such a fine, close weave that stains cannot penetrate to the reverse side. Their linings of firm checked material are equally resistant to time and wear.

This Burberry was taken to pieces, soaked in a biological detergent, washed and ironed. The wrong sides of the fabric and lining were as good as new.

The dismembered coat gave plenty of fabric for a boy's anorak. This particular style was chosen because it demonstrates the most awkward problem of pattern placing that you would encounter. The wide-topped raglan sleeve, and the large hood and pocket pieces, are difficult to fit in on the coat, especially if there are long pocket openings to be avoided. The anorak shown was in a boy's Size 8; but you would be able to cut up to a Size 12 from the available fabric if there were no hood, and if the sleeve shape corresponded more nearly to the original one.

8 (Opposite) A boy's anorak made from a man's raincoat (see this page)

Lay the pattern pieces right side up on the right-hand *inside* of the garment, and cut them out. Then reverse all the patterns, and lay them printed-side-down on the left-hand side of the garment. You will not need to cut a second back-neck facing (figure 6.58).

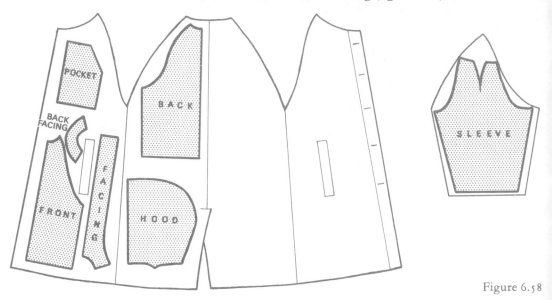

Figure 6.58

For the lining, lay the patterns in the same positions on the old lining. The back, front and sleeve patterns only will be needed – not the facings or pocket. The hood of this anorak was lined with fabric from an old scarlet T-shirt, which also made a piping for the pockets.

You would of course use a bought paper pattern, and follow its instructions; but if none were given for a lining, make it as follows:

1 Make up the back, front and sleeves of the lining.
2 Make up the back, front and sleeves of the anorak, and set on the pockets.
3 Make and line the hood. Finish its front edge.
4 Put the lining in place inside the anorak, wrong sides together.
5 Fold back the anorak front edge, and tack its side-seam turnings to the lining turnings to prevent the lining from slipping (figure 6.59).

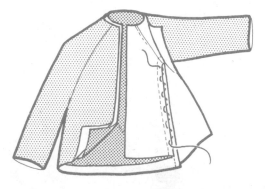

Figure 6.59

6 Tack lining and outer fabric together round the neckline, down the fronts and round the lower edge. From there on, treat the two fabrics as one, sewing on the hood, facings and zip through both thicknesses.

7 Turn up the hem to enclose the edge of the lining.

The anorak illustrated has sleeve straps. These were added simply to hide snagged threads left by the sleeve buttons on the old coat: an example of where a cover-up can actually add to the style of the garment.

Skirt into Pedal-Pushers

Almost any washable skirt fabric – denim, flannel or jersey – would be suitable for these little pants. Wool jersey was used for the ones shown in illustration 9 (see page 105) and figure 6.60.

Figure 6.60

An adult's skirt would probably be long enough to make into trousers for a child up to Size 4: in larger sizes, you could not get the leg length needed. However, it is perfectly possible to cut mid-calf pedal-pushers in sizes up to 8, or even 10, from a plain A-line skirt.

The pattern pieces will fit best on the skirt if they are laid upside-down, the trouser-waist of the pattern being placed to the hem of the skirt. If the skirt is not quite wide enough, overlap the back and front pieces of the pattern along the side seam (matching the seamlines), and cut out as one piece. You would lose a little shaping at the hip if these edges were not absolutely straight in the first place; but in a child's trousers, this is of little importance, and saving on the seam turnings may give you the little extra width of fabric needed (figure 6.61).

Figure 6.61

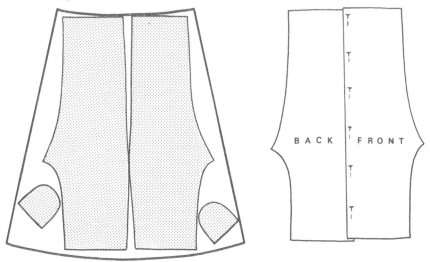

BACK FRONT

Evening Dress into Bridesmaid's or Party Dress

Even the narrowest evening dress would give plenty of fabric for this transformation (see illustration 10, page 115). Dark or brilliant colours suit little girls beautifully – especially if sparked with lace. You would need a bought paper pattern. For a stiff fabric, choose a pattern with a slightly flared skirt: for a sheer fabric, a skirt with gathers from the yoke or waist would be better (figure 6.62).

So far as possible, cut the pieces from the corresponding ones of the larger dress. Puffed sleeves cut on the cross, to give them a softer line, take up a good deal of fabric: they also need a small sleeve-lining to hold them well puffed up. A layout is suggested in figure 6.63, but the cut of the original dress may influence the placing of some smaller pieces.

ATTACHING THE LACE

You will need 1.2 metres of lace. Before assembling the dress, tack a strip of lace along the waistline of each skirt panel, placing it 1 cm below the edge. Tack the bodice section over the lace and skirt, and machine 1.5 cm from the edges (figure 6.64).

The neckline lace should be sewn on after the facings are attached, but before catching them down to the seams inside the dress. Cut a strip of lace 1½ times the length of the neckline – about 50 cm. Gather the lace down the middle, draw it up to fit, and back-stitch it in place by hand, over the gathering thread, just below the finished neckline.

Figure 6.62

Figure 6.63

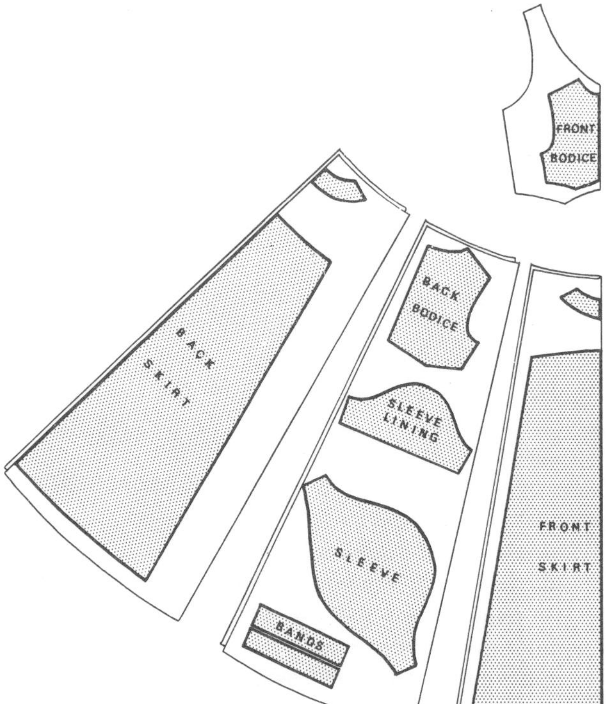

Do not catch in the facing. If the lace is very narrow, two widths can be used, just overlapped and sewn together with the gathering thread (figure 6.65).

THE DOROTHY BAG

This little bag would complete the outfit. Make it from scraps. The base of the bag should be stiffened with a circle of card (figure 6.66).

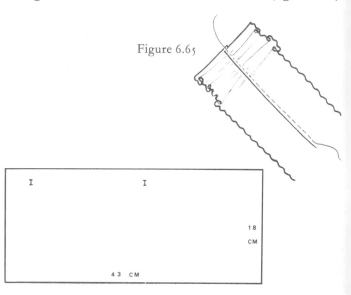

Figure 6.65

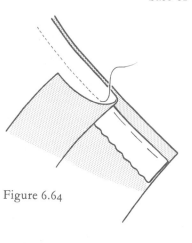

Figure 6.64

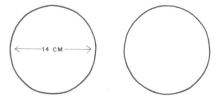

Figure 6.66

1 Make two small buttonholes (page 47), 2 cm down from the top edge of the rectangle. Or pierce holes, and tightly overcast their edges.
2 Stitch the side seam of the bag.
3 Turn in and machine a 3 cm hem along the top edge, to form a casing for the draw strings.
4 For the base of the bag, stitch the two circles together round half their circumference, turn them right side out, and slip a slightly smaller card circle between the layers. Turn in the raw edges round the rest of the base, and sew together with the drawing stitch shown on page 20.
5 Fold in a narrow turning round the lower edge of the bag. Pin this fold to the base of the bag, and draw-stitch firmly together.
6 Cut two 50 cm lengths of silky cord and thread them, from opposite buttonholes, through the casing. Knot the ends.

9 (Opposite) Pedal-pushers made from a skirt (see page 101)

7 Taking a Pattern from a Garment

When you are remodelling clothes, a new commercial paper pattern may well seem an undue expense. There are several other ways of obtaining patterns, either for a whole garment or for part of one.

It is surprisingly easy to draft one's own block patterns for the basic shapes of bodice, skirt or sleeve. These can be used many times over, adapting them to the currently fashionable line. One of the several excellent books on pattern drafting would be an investment for the serious dressmaker.

Or, if you have unpicked a garment completely, the separate pieces can of course be used as a pattern. Each piece should first be pressed along the straight grain of the fabric, to make sure that it is free from distortion. Draw round the outlines, over brown paper, and you will have a complete pattern for future use.

However, most renovations and remodellings do not need whole patterns. It is often more practical to take a pattern just of the section needed, from the garment itself. This is normally done on a dress-stand – using muslin or calico for the pattern; putting it over the garment section; and pinning any dart shapings directly on to the muslin. This is not always easy, because the straight grain of garment and muslin must be kept exactly matching.

But patterns can equally well be transferred from the garment directly to squared dressmaker's paper; or with careful measuring, to brown paper. For beginners, this method may well prove more accurate than using muslin, as it gives a very near approximation to the garment section. It is actually the simpler method, and is the one described here. For completeness, all the basic shapes of bodice, sleeve and skirt are given. In practice, though, one is more often likely to use patterns for the smaller parts, such as collars and facings. Work on a large table, with room for your garment and pattern paper to be laid out side by side.

Front Bodice Pattern Fold the bodice down its centre front, exactly on the straight thread of the fabric, with the right-hand half of the bodice uppermost. Take these measurements from the bodice, and plot them in the same order on your paper (figure 7.1).

BODICE   PATTERN   Figure 7.1

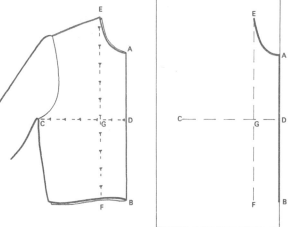

1 Centre-front length of the bodice, A–B. Mark this length along the right-hand edge of the paper.
2 Underarm width across the bodice, from where the side seam meets the armhole, to the centre front. Measure exactly along the horizontal thread, and mark with a line of pins. Call this line C–D.
3 Measure A–D on the bodice. Take the same measurement downwards from A on the pattern, and mark in D. Draw the line D–C at right angles to A–B, the same length as D–C on the garment.
4 On the bodice, mark a line with pins from the neck end of the shoulder seam, down to the waistline (E–F). Keep it parallel to A–B, along the straight grain of the fabric, crossing C–D at G.
5 Measure D–G. Transfer this measurement to the pattern, marking G on the line between D and C. Draw the line E–G–F, parallel to A–B. Make E–G and G–F the same lengths as on the bodice. On these three lines, the rest of the pattern is built.
6 Place the bodice over the paper pattern, matching points E and A, and draw in the neckline curve, using the bodice neckline to guide your pencil. If there is a collar in the way, simply match points E and A, and prick with a needle through the seamline, leaving a row of pricked holes in the paper underneath. Join these up with pencil. Or use dressmaker's carbon paper and a tracing wheel.
7 If there are no darts, continue to draw in the bodice outline (figure 7.2). First, match the bodice centre front, A–B, to the pattern; then match points E and C. Draw in the shoulder seamline, and the curve round the armhole, down to C (dotted line).
8 Now, matching centre fronts and point C, draw in the underarm seam and the waistline.
9 Add 1.5 cm seam allowances along all the edges of the pattern except for the centre front.
10 Mark in a grain-arrow parallel to the right-hand edge of the pattern.
11 Cut out the pattern along the solid lines.

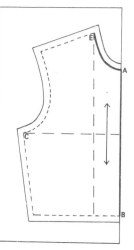

Figure 7.2

DEALING WITH DARTS

So far, we have been copying on the flat. However, there is almost certain to be at least one dart to give shape to the bodice.

If there is a shoulder dart Carry out Steps 1 to 6 above. Then continue, consulting figure 7.3:

Figure 7.3

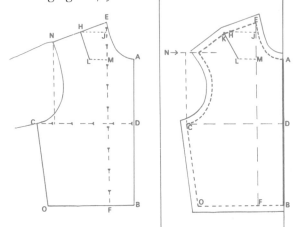

7 On the bodice, measure from the upper end of the dart, H, across to J, on the line E–F. Keep this measurement parallel to C–D; J will fall just below E. Measure E–J.

8 On the pattern, measure the same length from E down to J. At this level, mark in the line J–H, parallel to D–C. Join E–H, to give the shoulder seamline as far as the dart.

9 Measure the width of the dart where it joins the shoulder seam, from stitching to the fold of the dart (figure 7.4). Add this measurement to the line E–H on the pattern, to end at K; K gives the centre of the dart.

10 Now measure the bodice from the lower point of the dart, L, across to M, on the line E–F. Measure E–M.

11 Transfer the measurement E–M to the pattern and mark in M.

12 Transfer the measurement M–L to the pattern, and mark in L. Join K–L to give the fold line of the dart.

13 On the bodice, measure from the line C–D up to the armhole end of the shoulder seam, N. Mark this *level* on the pattern, using a horizontal line the same distance above C, to represent N for the moment.

14 Now, on the bodice, measure the length of the shoulder seam from dart to armhole, H–N, and add to this the width of the dart, as before. This measurement will give the distance on the *pattern* from the centre of the dart, K, along the shoulder to the armhole. Draw in the K–N measurement, to meet at an angle the line you have already drawn for the level of N. (This part of the seamline will not continue as a straight line with E–K, but will slope slightly downwards. When the dart is stitched, the shoulder line will be straightened up.)

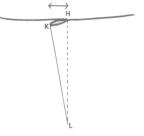

Figure 7.4

15 Now place the bodice over the pattern, and draw in the curve
 N–C, using the garment armhole to guide you.
16 With the bodice still over the pattern, match the centre fronts down
 to B. Draw the waistline, B–F–O, using the waist seamline to guide
 you.
17 On the pattern, join C–O to give the side seam.
18 Add seam allowances of 1.5 cm and grain-arrow, as before, and
 cut out.

If there is an underarm dart Carry out Steps 1–6 above. Now continue, consulting figure 7.5 :

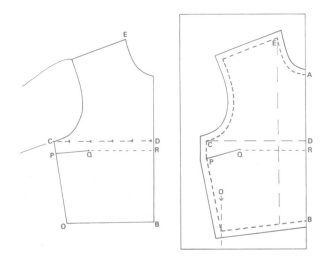

Figure 7.5

7 Match the bodice to the pattern at E and C. Draw in the shoulder
 seamline, and the curve round the armhole down to C.
8 On the bodice, measure the side seam from the armhole to the wide
 end of the dart, C–P, and add the width of the dart from stitching to
 fold.
9 Transfer this whole measurement to the pattern, drawing the line
 C–P straight downwards from C.
10 Measure the bodice width from the centre front, along the waistline, to the side seam (B–O).
11 On the pattern, mark the length B–O, using a vertical line to represent O for the moment.
12 Measure the side seam of the bodice from the dart to the waistline,
 P–O, and add to this the width of the dart from stitching to fold.
13 Transfer this whole measurement to the pattern, marking a line
 from P to meet the O line at an angle. This, like the shoulder dart,
 will give a cranked edge which will be straightened up when the
 dart is stitched. Mark in the line O–B.
14 On the bodice, measure from the point of the dart, Q, across to the
 centre front Q–R. Measure the distance of R below D, and transfer
 this measurement to the pattern. Then measure back to Q to give
 the end of the dart.

15 Add seam allowances of 1.5 cm along all edges of the pattern except the centre front. Mark in a grain-arrow, and cut out.

If there is an under-bust dart Carry out Steps 1–6 above. Now continue, consulting figure 7.6:

Figure 7.6

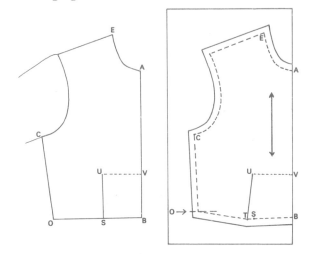

7 Match the bodice to the pattern at E and C. Draw in the shoulder seamline, and the curve round the armhole down to C.

8 Measure the bodice side seam, C–O. Mark this measurement on the pattern, using a horizontal line to represent O for the moment.

9 Lay the bodice over the pattern, matching centre fronts. Draw in the waistline from B to the base of the dart, S. To this line, add the width of the dart from stitching to fold. Mark this point T – it will be the centre of the dart.

10 On the bodice, measure from the base of the dart to the side seam, S–O. Add to this the width of the dart.

11 On the pattern, draw in this measurement T–O, from T towards the left, meeting the O line at a slight angle. Join C–O.

12 On the bodice, measure from the point of the dart to the centre-front, U–V. Measure the distance of V above B, and plot V on the pattern. Measure back to give the position of U, the upper end of the dart. Join U–T to give the fold-line.

13 Add seam allowances and grain-arrow, as before.

Back Bodice Pattern Take the pattern from the right-hand side of the back bodice. You will then have a complete right-hand half of the bodice, to which a sleeve or collar can be fitted.

Work in exactly the same way as for the front bodice, including any shoulder or waistline darts. The centre-back line will come at the left-hand edge of the paper pattern.

Sleeve Pattern Fold the right sleeve along its centre line from shoulder seam to hem. The fold should be on the straight grain of the fabric, opposite to the underarm seam. Now proceed, consulting figure 7.7:

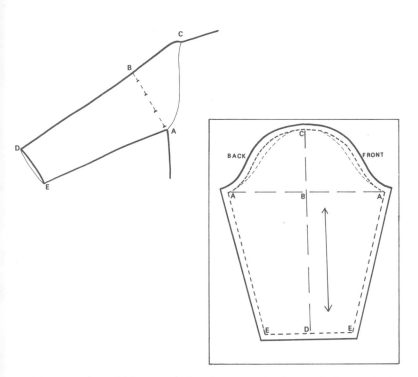

Figure 7.7

1 Measure the width round the sleeve at the base of the armhole, keeping along the straight thread (A–B–A). Mark this with a line of pins.

2 Mark this length horizontally across your paper, marking in B at the centre.

3 On the sleeve, measure down the fold from shoulder seamline, C, to B; then on down to D at the hem. Transfer these measurements to the pattern, keeping C–B–D at right angles to A–B–A.

4 Measure round the sleeve hem, E–D–E, and transfer this measurement to the pattern.

5 Measure the length of the underarm seam A–E, and check that it matches A–E on the pattern. Draw in these lines.

6 If there is an elbow dart, allow for the width of this on the left-hand edge of the pattern; the line from D to E at the left of the pattern will then slope downwards.

7 Place the folded sleeve over the pattern and draw in the back and front curves at the sleevehead, A–C and C–A. These will not be identical, so mark the back and front edges on the pattern.

8 Measure the width across the sleevehead, 5 cm down from C. This will be a little greater than the corresponding width you have marked on the pattern, because the sleeve will have been *gathered* into the armhole. So adjust the curve A–C–A on the pattern, to allow for this extra width.

9 Mark 1.5 cm seam allowances on all edges of the pattern – or more at the lower end of the sleeve, if a hem is needed. Draw in a grain-arrow.

Skirt Pattern Using the right-hand side of the skirt, make a pattern for the half-front, consulting figure 7.8:

1 Fold the skirt down its centre front, A–B. Measure the finished length, and mark it along the right-hand edge of the paper.
2 Lay the skirt over the pattern, matching A–B, and draw in the waistline curve as far as the dart, C. (If there is no dart, simply draw in the whole waistline.)
3 With the skirt still on the pattern, draw in the hemline from centre front to side seam, B–D, using the skirt hem to guide you.
4 Measure the width of the dart from stitching to fold, and add this measurement to A–C, ending at E.
5 On the skirt, measure the waistline from the dart to the side seam, C–F. Add to this measurement the width of the dart. Transfer this whole measurement, E–F, to the pattern, using a vertical line to represent F for the moment.
6 Lay the skirt on the pattern, matching the lower end of the side seam to D on the pattern. Arrange the seam so that its waistline end meets the line F. Draw in the seam, being careful to keep exact the shaping over the hip.

Figure 7.8

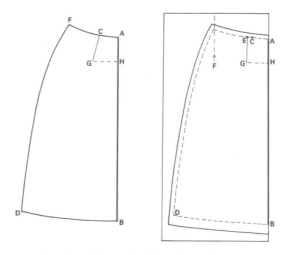

7 Join E–F, using the skirt waistline to guide you if the curve is pronounced.
8 On the skirt, measure from the point of the dart, G, to the centre front, H, keeping along the straight grain of the fabric. Measure the distance of H below A.
9 Transfer the measurement A–H to the pattern, and measure back to plot the position of G. G–E is the centre-line of the dart.
10 Add seam allowances of 1.5 cm along the side and waist edges of the pattern, and 5 cm (or more, as necessary) along the hem edge. Cut out the pattern along the solid lines.

The half-back pattern is made in just the same way, with the centre-back line at the left-hand edge of the paper.

Facings are cut from the same pattern as the garment section they are **Facings Patterns** to face. To make a facing pattern:

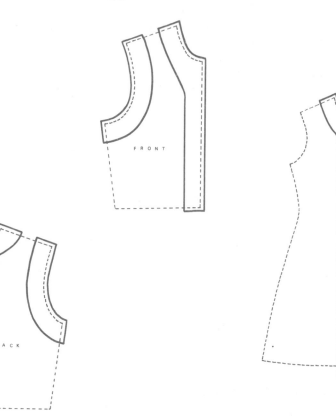

Figure 7.9

1 First make a paper pattern of the garment section itself.
2 Now place a sheet of tissue paper over the garment pattern, and trace through it the line of the edge to be faced. (Shown in figure 7.9 by dotted lines.)
3 The width of a facing should be:
    along the front edge – at least 7 cm
    round a neckline   – at least 5 cm
    round an armhole   – 5 cm.
4 Draw the inner edge of the facing parallel to the garment edge just traced, up as far as the top-button level. Then slant the line away up to the shoulder seamline. Keep all curves an even distance from the edge of the garment pattern.
5 Along the shoulder, neckline, armhole and front edges, add seam allowances of 1.5 cm. At the hem edge add up to 5 cm, or the depth of the garment hem.
6 Mark in a fold-arrow at the centre-back of a neckline facing, to show that the pattern piece must be placed to a fold of the fabric when being cut out.
7 Cut out the facing patterns along the solid lines.

Collar Patterns The neck edge of a collar must be cut to fit the neck of the garment. This obvious fact is easy to forget; but if one has to alter the neck of a dress, then the collar pattern will also have to be altered. Find the neck measurement by placing the back and front bodice patterns so that they match along the shoulder line. It is then simple to take the centre-back to centre-front measurement (figure 7.10).

Once the neck edge is determined, the free edge of the collar can be drawn to whatever shape and depth the fashion line of the moment may suggest.

Figure 7.10

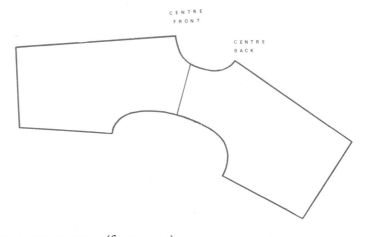

MANDARIN COLLARS (figure 7.11)
Cut a straight strip of paper 4 cm deep and the length of the neckline from centre-back to centre-front. To let the collar lie close to the neck, its upper edge must be shortened. 5 cm from the centre-back, crease and pin a dart 1 cm wide at the upper edge, tapering to nothing at the neck seamline. Midway between this dart and the centre-front, crease and pin another 1 cm dart. To prevent the ends of the collar from overlapping, trim 1 cm from the upper edge at the centre-front, making a sloping end; round off the corner (figure 7.12).

Figure 7.11

Figure 7.12

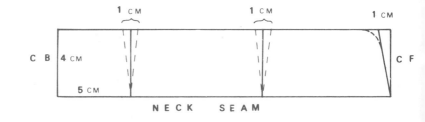

10 (Opposite) A girl's party dress made from an evening dress (see page 102)

On another sheet of paper, trace round the outline of the altered pattern. Mark in a fold-arrow at centre-back. Add seam allowances of 1.5 cm at the upper, lower and centre-front edges (figure 7.13). Cut out along the solid lines.

Figure 7.13

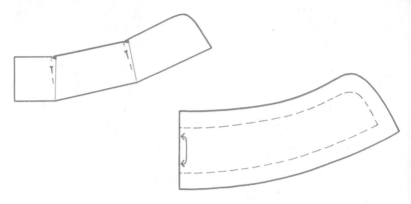

Figure 7.14

TIE COLLARS

These are simply straight strips, joined at the centre-back. They can be as little as 4 cm wide; but strips 7 cm wide will allow the collar to be turned down round the neck, and will give a more substantial bow.

For a flip-over tie, the strips should be 60 cm long; for a bow, allow 75 cm. Add seam allowances of 1.5 cm on all four edges.

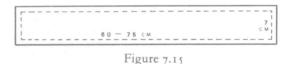

Figure 7.15

Four strips of fabric will be needed for this collar, as it is made in double thickness, and seamed at centre-back. (Figure 7.15.)

ROLLED COLLARS

Collars can be cut to lie quite flat to the back and shoulders. But they look better if they stand up from the seam, and frame the neck more closely. The higher the collar is to stand, the wider it must be from the neck seamline to the free edge. By adjusting this width, a collar can be designed to roll at whatever height you wish.

1 Lay the front and back bodice patterns on a sheet of brown paper, so that they match along the shoulder seam (figure 7.16).
2 Draw in the centre-back, neckline and centre-front edges on the paper. If there is a front opening with an overlap for buttoning, fold in the overlap and draw down the centre-front marking (7.17).
3 Remove the pattern pieces. Draw in on the paper the style line for the outer edge of the collar. This should begin at right angles to the centre-back, and should give a depth of at least 5–6 cm, more if the stand is to be very high. The whole character of the collar depends on this line – whether a narrow, neat Peter Pan or an extravagant, Byronic collar with wide-set points (figure 7.18).
4 Add 1.5 cm along the neck edge, as shown by the dotted line (7.19), and cut out the collar shape. (Add more than 1.5 cm if you want a higher stand to the collar.) The neck edge will now be too short to fit the neckline, so slash the pattern at A, B and C (figure 7.20), and

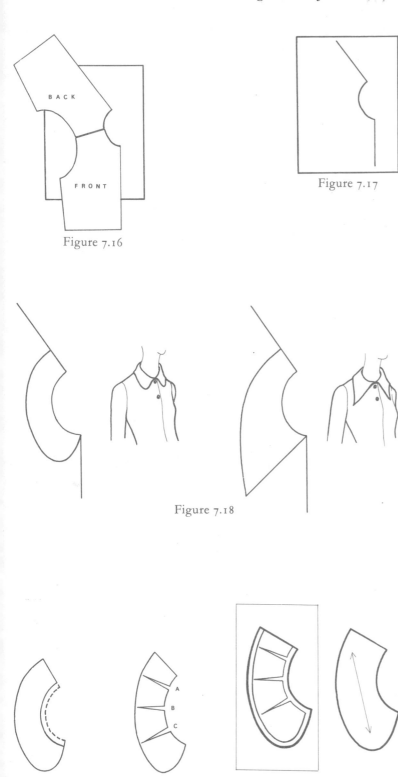

Figure 7.16

Figure 7.17

Figure 7.18

Figure 7.19

Figure 7.20

Figure 7.21

Figure 7.22

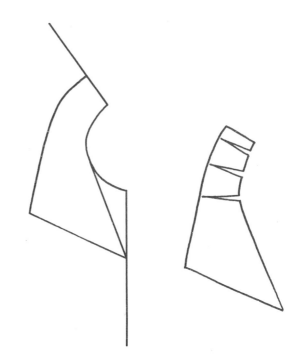

open it out until it does fit. You will need to add nearly 1 cm at each slash. The outer edge of the collar, the style line, is not altered.

5 Pin the pattern to another piece of paper, add seam allowances of 1.5 cm all round except at the centre-back, and cut round its new edge (figure 7.21). Mark in a straight grain arrow as shown, at an angle of 45 degrees to the centre-back of the collar.

6 For a lower neckline at the front, simply draw in the neckline of the collar as a line straight down from the shoulder seam to the centre-front (figure 7.22). Then make the same alterations as above.

This method of giving a raised roll to the collar is better than the one usually shown in pattern-drafting books, as it preserves the full width of the collar.

8 Precious Old Fabrics

Any fine old textiles you may have put away – silks, laces, embroideries, christening robes – must certainly be interesting, or you would not have kept them. They might prove to be rare and important, even if of no great monetary value. Fine old lace used to command high prices, right up to the 1939–45 war; when commercial interest in it flagged, the major London salerooms dropped their lace sales. Only very recently has interest revived, and lace is again becoming saleable.

This chapter discusses the best methods of storing such pieces, how they can safely be cleaned and cared for, and in what ways they could be used or displayed. To begin with a caution: you can do irreversible damage to delicate old fabrics by careless handling or unconsidered treatment. Even though linen and cotton sometimes retain their strength almost indefinitely, silk tends to rot, particularly when it has been exposed to sunlight. You should therefore handle silk with the greatest care, expecting it to be frail. Do not attempt to restore *any* textile unless you are quite sure that you know the fibre it is composed of, and the treatment suitable both for that fibre and for the condition of the fabric.

Museums can help you in identifying fabrics, and in dating garments. If you have something worth preserving, but do not want to keep it yourself, a museum might well be grateful for its loan or gift. (Old wedding dresses are usually welcomed, as they can be dated with certainty.) But it is not generally realized that Costume and Textile Departments are interested in much more than preserving ancient pieces. Their collections are continually being brought up to date, to include for example the 'sack' styles of the early 1960s and the cheesecloth-top-and-jeans uniform of the 1970s, along with shoes and other accessories. A list of museums with Costume Departments is given at the end of this chapter: do consult the Keeper of Textiles at your nearest museum, for identification and advice.

Museums might undertake restoration work for you. They are unlikely, however, to give any advice on how you could treat a piece yourself, for fear that you might damage it. Yet it seems sensible to know what one can safely do – on the analogy of rendering first aid – rather than cause harm by wrong handling, or through ill-guided experimentation. Indeed, to store fabrics in a dirty or dusty condition can in itself be very damaging. The methods and cleaning agents detailed here are those which, with proper care, one can safely use to treat old fabrics.

The Problems There are really five problems. The fibres themselves may be weak or rotten – in which case the way they are stored and handled may affect their life. The fabric may be dirty or generally discoloured. It may be spotted with brown marks. It may be limp and lifeless. Or it may need mending.

The most important point of all is that fabrics should be properly supported while you work on them. Fibres weakened by age or sunlight can be further damaged by any strain put on the fabric as a whole. So avoid lifting fragile pieces by one edge, or shaking them out. Most especially, avoid handling them unsupported while they are wet. They should always be spread on a larger piece of fabric – or polythene – to prevent any strain while lifting them.

The dust of ages may be gently removed by using suction from the hand-held nozzle of a cylinder-type vacuum cleaner. This can make a quite remarkable difference to the colour of pile fabrics or wool embroideries.

Washing Any water used on old textiles must be soft. Distilled water is ideal. (The brown marks on old linens and laces are often caused by a residue of iron, left after washing in hard water.) If a fabric is patterned or coloured, you would be unwise to attempt washing it without expert advice. Some dyes may not be fast even in cold water. But white or natural-coloured fabrics, if washable at all, will be safe in luke-warm water. Test first at an inconspicuous point.

Do not use soap. It is slightly alkaline, and so may be damaging to silk; and it may leave a dull film over the fibres. It is better to use a mild detergent, which is more nearly neutral and which leaves no deposit. Here, one must distinguish between the heavy-duty detergents designed for washing-up or general laundry-work, which contain bleaching or oxidizing agents; and the mild detergents intended for the hand-washing of wool. It could be most harmful to use the former on any old fabric whatever – so avoid any detergent recommended for washing machines. Use preparations designed especially for delicate fabrics, such as Stergene. (Museums use Lisapol N, obtainable from Frank Joel, Museum Suppliers, Norwich.)

Silk Old silks can be especially fragile, as both sunlight and alkalis tend to rot them. Past washings may have taken their toll. Handle them with the greatest care.

STAIN REMOVAL
Grease stains should respond to white spirit. Lay the stained part face down over a pad of white fabric, and work from the back of the silk, gently applying the spirit on swabs of cotton wool, and moving from

outside the stain towards the centre. For iron rust stains, 1% oxalic acid may be dropped (with an eye-dropper) on the mark. Leave for a minute or so, and rinse with cool water. If this has no effect, use acetic acid (0.5%) in the same way. Be sure to rinse thoroughly.

WASHING

Many silks are not washable at all. Do not attempt to wash heavy satins or brocades. But a thin silk such as crêpe-de-chine is washable. The type of garment could be the best guide: silk blouses and under-wear were meant to be washed – other garments usually not.

Wash in luke-warm water with Stergene or a similar preparation. (Soda, being alkaline, should never be used; nor should any biological detergent.) Handle the silk as little as possible. To give support while it is wet, place it in a pillow-case, immerse, and gently squeeze and stroke it through the pillow-case. Rinse several times, then extract the silk and roll it in a white towel. Leave for an hour or two, by which time it will be in the right state for ironing – very slightly but evenly damp.

STIFFENING

Some silk fabrics are improved by a little stiffening. Use gum arabic, which is especially suitable for silk. To make gum arabic, add ½ litre of cold water to 30 grams of powdered gum arabic (1 pint to 1 oz). Heat until the gum has dissolved completely. To each part of this solution, add ten parts of hot water. Allow to cool, and use. (This mixture will not keep.) Immerse the damp silk in this solution, then roll it in a towel as above, and iron.

IRONING

Iron on the wrong side with a cool iron (setting no. 1). Silk scorches easily, and an over-hot iron can leave a shiny patch. Be very careful not to get any drops of water on the silk; they would leave spot-marks which could only be removed by re-wetting the whole piece, rolling it in a towel again, and re-ironing.

Fine Linens and Cotton Lawns

Christening robes and baby dresses, encrusted with white embroidery or broderie anglaise, lavished with lace – these beautiful heirlooms can be preserved indefinitely with proper care.

STAIN REMOVAL

Iron rust marks can be removed in the same way as from silk; but the treatment with oxalic acid could be a little more prolonged. Or use lemon juice, well rinsed with warm water, before washing the whole piece. Grease stains should respond to washing.

WASHING

Wash by hand in Stergene (or a similar product), as for silk. Hand-hot rather than luke-warm water can be used.

STIFFENING

These fabrics can be lightly starched, following the directions on the packet. If a starched finish is not wanted, a fabric conditioner such as Comfort is quite safe. The manufacturers are confident that it can have no long-term ill-effects. Comfort will restore body to a fabric, and even give bulk to flattened cotton fibres.

IRONING

Iron slightly damp, on the wrong side, at setting no. 1 or 2. Do not use more heat than necessary. Embroidered materials should be ironed on a padded board, to allow the surface to stand out in good relief.

Fine Old Lace

Hand-made lace consists of fine, tightly-twisted linen threads. It was never white; its natural colour ranged from cream or ivory to ecru, and often it was dyed slightly darker in weak tea or coffee. So any bleaching could not only weaken the threads, but also ruin its whole character. Do not think, for instance, of bleaching an old lace flounce so as to use it on a wedding dress; but instead choose the dress fabric to match the lace.

The cleaning of old lace is not a job to be undertaken lightly. It demands skill, patience and a great deal of time. The Misses Rosa and Louisa Tebbs, who taught lace-making at the end of the last century, wrote that lace-cleaning was 'a source of occupation gladly welcomed by reduced gentlewomen, who can follow it at their homes and add a considerable amount to their straitened incomes'. We have wider opportunities these days, perhaps; but certainly less time.

STAIN REMOVAL

Small brownish marks, if grease-based, should respond to washing in Stergene and warm water. Iron-mould spots should be treated with oxalic acid and if necessary with acetic acid, as for iron-mould on silk. Always wash lace after this treatment.

Another method is with lemon juice. First, spread the section of lace over a pad of white cotton or linen. Damp the spot with a drop of water. Then work in a few drops of lemon juice, using a soft paint-brush. Keep the treatment just over the spot – do not let the surrounding area of lace get wet. When the stain has faded, rinse well by dripping plain water over the spot, and frequently changing the pad under the lace. In this way, a mark can be treated without washing the whole piece of lace.

WASHING

Wind the lace round your hand, into a flat pad. Then tack it through all its thicknesses, to hold it together and support it during washing. If the lace is fragile, instead of tacking it put it into a bag made from a handkerchief or from muslin, and wash it in that. A small, curved piece, such as a collar or the lace from a fan, could be tacked flat to polythene, to keep it in shape and support it.

Wash in Stergene and hand-hot, soft water, stroking and gently squeezing the lace. (For silk laces, such as Maltese, the water should be no more than luke-warm.) The old method, recommended in Thérèse de Dillmont's *Encyclopedia of Needlework*, was to wind lace round a bottle, sew a muslin covering over it, and boil it for an hour in soap and several changes of water; this is not to be recommended now that we have safe detergents that work at lower temperatures, more effectively. Rinse very thoroughly. Roll the lace (still supported by tacking, bag or polythene) in a dry towel, and leave for a couple of hours.

STIFFENING
Use a gum arabic solution, in the same way as for silk. The strength of the solution may be increased by adding only 5 to 8 parts of water, instead of 10, to the original mix. Immerse the damp lace in this, before rolling it in a towel.

PINNING OUT
Cover a well-padded ironing board with a piece of white cloth. Unroll the lace a little at a time. With stainless steel pins, pin it out on the ironing board. Place the pins close together, to keep straight the heading of the lace. Along the shaped edge, pin out through its loop each single, separate picot. This is extremely time-consuming; do not begin it unless you are sure of being able to work without interruption. If the lace dries before it is pinned out, pat it with a damp cloth.

It may now be left to dry naturally, or it may be dried more quickly with a hair-dryer. On no account iron it. Unpin only when you are sure it is quite dry.

Store the clean lace by winding it round a card, and wrapping it in tissue paper. To put it into a polythene bag would be to invite mildew.

Coarse Laces

Torchon, Nottingham, machine-made and crochet laces can simply be folded over and supported by your hand during washing. Wash in Stergene and hand-hot water, rinse well, and leave rolled in a towel for an hour or so. There is seldom any need to pin out these coarse laces. They can safely be ironed on a well-padded ironing board. Lay the lace face down, cover it with a sheet of tissue paper, and iron at setting no. 1, or for very thick lace at no. 2 as for wool. The right side of the lace will come up with the pattern in good relief.

Net, Tulle and Dress Lace Flouncing

Do not try to wash any of these; they are difficult to handle when wet, the mesh of net becomes distorted, and it is almost impossible to get a large area back into shape. But they can be freshened and stiffened without washing. Lay the dry net on the ironing board – or better still on a table covered with a blanket and a sheet. Lay over the net a piece of white lawn or muslin, wrung out in the gum arabic solution, as above. Press the net through the lawn. When quite dry and crisp, move on to the next section.

Beaded Fabrics Damaged parts of a beaded or sequinned dress present a problem, because the weight of the beads may have torn or weakened the material itself. So treat any such garment as extremely frail.

Before touching the beads, make sure that the foundation on which they are sewn is sound. If not, you should attempt no more than just to hold the foundation fabric together with a piece of chiffon, organza or net darned to the wrong side. Use a silk thread and a fine needle.

Any loose beads can then be re-sewn through to the new backing. Silk thread in a beading needle, size 10 or 12, will slip through the smallest beads. These needles bend easily: work gently. If the beads have been sewn on as a series, you may need to begin a few beads back, taking your thread through two or three that are still securely attached, and then continuing one by one with the loose beads. It is most unlikely that you could match any missing ones, nor is it desirable to add new to old. They would not look right, and their weight might do more damage.

Sequins or spangles may have been sewn on in an overlapping line. To re-attach them, follow their original placing with back-stitches, taking a sequin at each stitch. The thread will be hidden by the next sequin (figure 8.1).

Never attempt to wash or iron a beaded or sequinned dress; old sequins are made of a kind of gelatine, and can melt.

Storing Textiles Fabrics tend to be weakened along the lines of any sharp folds or creases. So if possible textiles should always be spread out quite flat for storage. Larger pieces (such as wedding veils) should be layered with tissue paper before folding; avoid storing heavier fabrics on top of them.

Another method is to roll the piece round a cylindrical cardboard core – dress fabric departments usually have plenty to spare.

Figure 8.1

Before putting them away, see that every piece is completely dry and in as clean a state as possible. Otherwise there may be trouble from mould or insects.

Display The opportunities for using family lace or old embroideries are limited virtually to christenings and weddings. So the problem of wear and damage to the fabric hardly arises. So long as no strain is placed on an old fabric, it would be a pity not to use it for what is after all its original purpose.

But many smaller pieces, which could not actually be worn, could be displayed rather than left unseen. The enemies are dust and sulphur dioxide, especially in the polluted atmosphere of towns. The latter is largely responsible for the tendering of fabrics. For protection, therefore, textiles should be mounted under glass or perspex. Do not display them where they can be reached by direct sunlight.

If the piece is without any raised pattern, it can be mounted simply between two sheets of glass, clipped together. But all embroideries, and any laces with a raised thread, are better mounted with a shallow

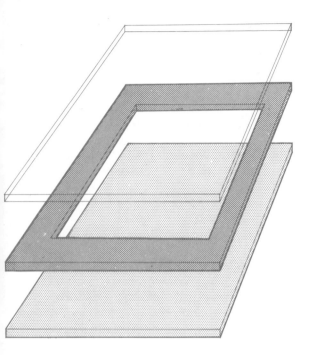

Figure 8.2

space under the glass. This is obtained by placing a fillet between the mounted fabric and the glass, all the layers being enclosed by the frame (figure 8.2).

Victorian frames with their original gold fillets can still be found; or one could use a card fillet, cut flush with the inner edge of the frame, to be invisible.

Unless the display will be horizontal, the textile must itself be mounted on a fabric backing, and this backing stretched over a board or card. A darker, contrasting material will show lace off particularly well. Any plain, finely-woven, matt-surfaced fabric would serve. Materials made of synthetic fibres, however, have the advantage of being both rot-proof and shrink-proof. Any textile mounted on these would be perfectly and indefinitely preserved. (It is becoming the practice to mount fragile old Regimental Colours between two layers of terylene net, rather than silk net as formerly, for this reason.)

First, stretch the backing in an embroidery frame. Then pin out the textile on it, and with a fine needle and polyester thread catch down single threads at even distances round the edge. On larger or heavier embroideries, stitches should also be made at intervals across the piece. Finally, the backing fabric is stretched over a board or card, ready for framing and glazing.

Museums with Costume and Textile Collections

BARNARD CASTLE *The Bowes Museum* (Durham County Council), DL1Z 8NP

BATH *Museum of Costume* (Bath City Council), Assembly Rooms, BA1 1LZ

The Costume and Fashion Research Centre (Bath City Council), Museum of Costume, 4 The Circus, BA1 2EW

The American Museum in Britain (Trustees of the American Museum), Claverton Manor, BA2 7BD: for American decorative arts, late 17th–mid 19th centuries

BEDFORD *Cecil Higgins Art Gallery* (Bedford District Council), Castle Close, MK40 3NY

BELFAST *Ulster Museum* (Ulster Museum Board of Trustees), Botanic Gardens, BT9 5AB: for advice. Their outstanding collection has been destroyed by fire

BIRMINGHAM *City Museum and Art Gallery* (City of Birmingham), Congreve Street, B3 4DH

BRIGHTON *Royal Pavilion*, Art Gallery & Museum (Borough of Brighton), BN1 1UE

BRISTOL *City Museum & Art Gallery* (Bristol District Council), Queen's Road, BS8 1RL

CAMBERLEY *National Army Museum* (Ministry of Defence), Royal Military Academy, Sandhurst: an outstation of the Museum in London

CAMBRIDGE *Fitzwilliam Museum* (University of Cambridge), Trumpington Street, CB2 1RB: only for textiles

CARDIFF *St Fagan's Welsh Folk Museum* (National Museum of Wales), St Fagan's Castle

COLCHESTER *Colchester & Essex Museum* (Colchester Borough Council), The Castle, CO1 1TJ

DOUGLAS *The Manx Museum* (Manx Museum & National Trust)

DUNDEE *City Museum & Art Gallery* (Dundee District Council), Albert Square, DD1 1DA: for advice, although the Museum does not specialize in textiles

DURHAM *Gulbenkian Museum of Oriental Art* (University of Durham), School of Oriental Studies, The University, Elvet Hill, DH1 3TH: for Chinese textiles

EDINBURGH *The Royal Scottish Museum* (National Museum), Chambers Street, EH1 1JF

EXETER *City Museum & Art Gallery* (Exeter City Council), Royal Albert Memorial Museum, Queen Street, EX4 3RX

GLASGOW *Art Gallery & Museum* (City of Glasgow District Council), Kelvingrove, G3 8AG

HARTLEBURY *Hereford & Worcester County Museum* (Hereford & Worcester County Council), Hartlebury Castle, Kidderminster DY11 7XZ

HEREFORD *Hereford City Museum* (Hereford District Council), Broad Street, HR4 9AU

IPSWICH *The Museum* (Borough of Ipswich), High Street, IP1 3QH

KENDAL *Abbot Hall Museum of Lakeland Life and Industry* (Lake District Museum Trust)